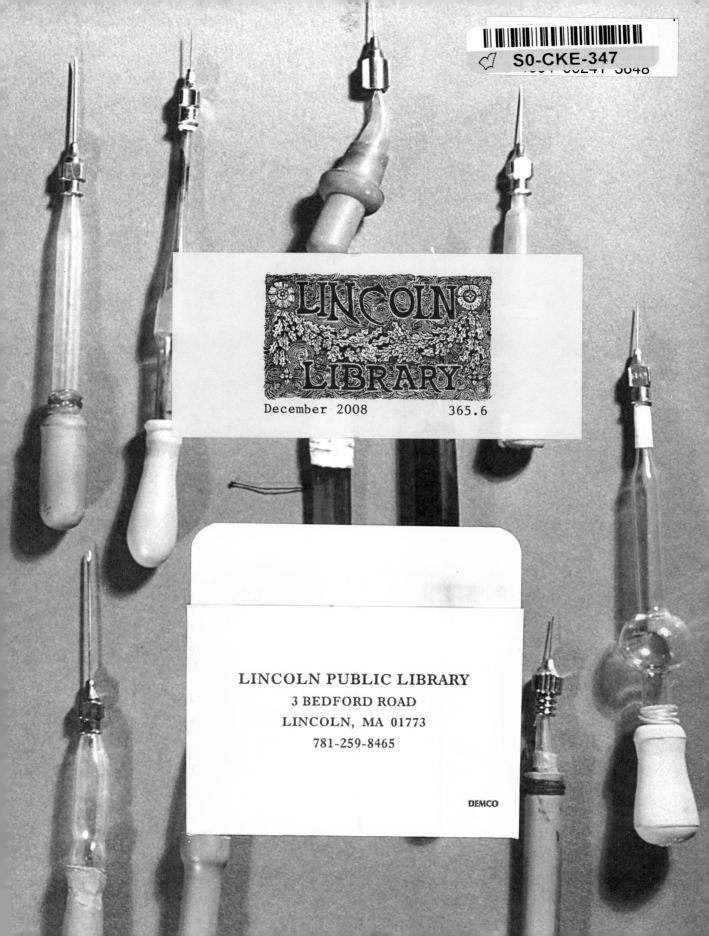

THE

United

UNITED

NARCOTI

A

LEXINGTO

INET SKETCHES -

FIRST

STATES
C FARM

KENTUCKY

FARM & PERSONNEL BLDGS.

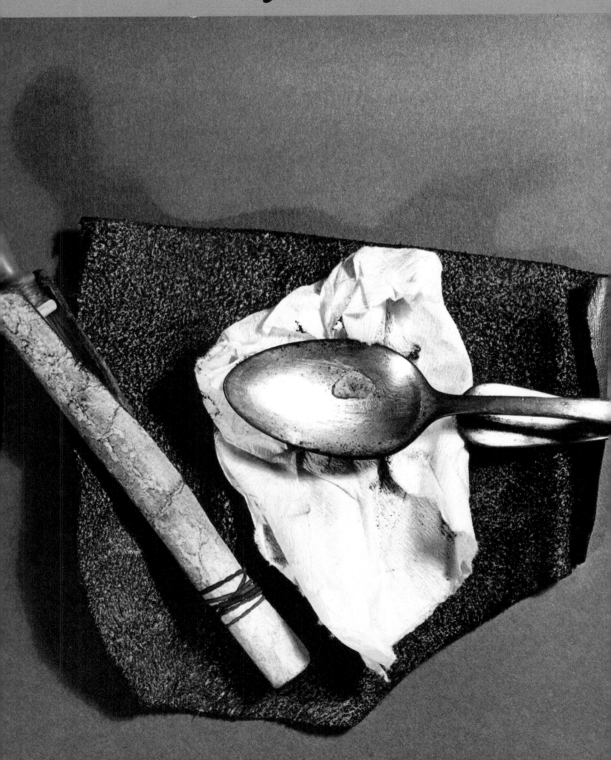

The Narcotic Farm

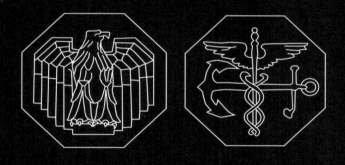

Nancy D. Campbell
JP Olsen
Luke Walden

Abrams, New York

Contents

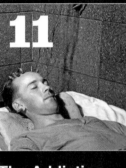

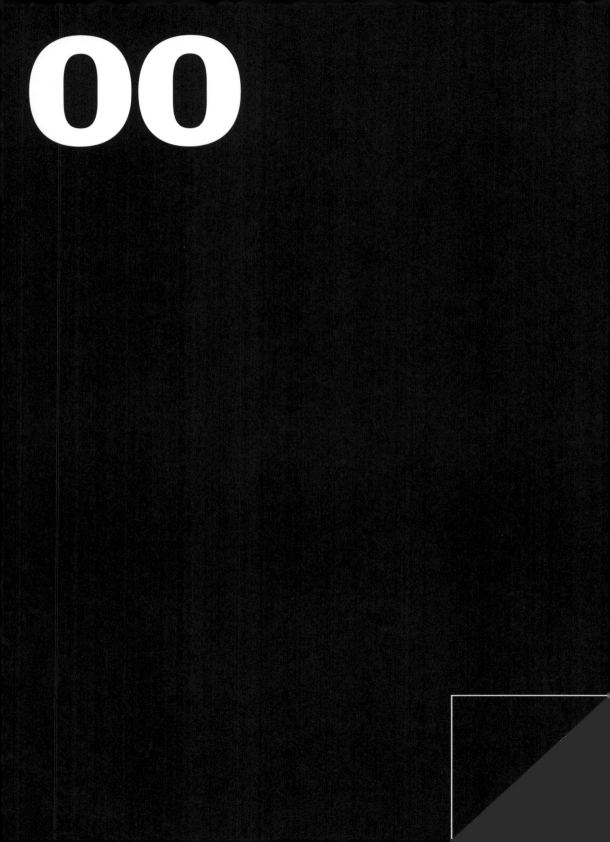

00

Introduction

The Narcotic Farm's goals were audacious: nothing less than the complete social rehabilitation of America's drug addicts and the discovery of a permanent cure for drug addiction. Today this dual mission seems hopelessly naive. But for decades these hopes animated the federal government's quest to solve the problem of drug addiction by confining the nation's addicts in one institution and transforming them into productive citizens.

From its opening in 1935, the Narcotic Farm epitomized the nation's ambivalence about how to deal with drug addiction. On the one hand, it functioned as a compassionate and humane hospital where addicts could recover from their drug habits. On the other hand, it was an imposing prison built to incarcerate drug addicts. Conceived and run jointly by the Bureau of Prisons and the Public Health Service, the Narcotic Farm—set on 1,000 acres of farmland just outside of Lexington, Kentucky—was an anomaly, an institution where male and female convicts arrested for drugs did time along with volunteers who checked themselves in for treatment. For both populations—which lived and worked together regardless of their legal status—going to Lexington meant they were "taking the cure."

"Narco," as it was known locally, housed a coed cast of strange bedfellows: heroin-addicted jazz musicians, opiate-abusing MDs and nurses, street hustlers and prostitutes from New York, and Dilaudid-addicted drugstore cowboys from the rural South were all in the mix. Described in the press as everything from a "New Deal for the Drug Addict" to a "million-dollar flophouse for junkies," the Narcotic Farm became a rite of passage for countless young addicts as well as the central gathering place for America's growing drug subculture.

The New Deal for the Drug Addict

In the 1920s, growing numbers of addicts started showing up at prisons across the country due to aggressive enforcement of the Harrison Narcotics Act and increasingly strict drug laws. Driven underground by law enforcement, the population of addicts that had formerly been comprised mostly of upper- and middle-class women addicted to pain medication now consisted almost entirely of working-class men hooked on illicit drugs. Police sent them to prison in droves. This new population of addict-inmates troubled wardens. Not only did they conspire to get drugs inside prisons, but they also introduced narcotics to non-addict inmates. As addicts continued to be arrested in record numbers, the prison population skyrocketed; and by the late 1920s a third of all federal prisoners were doing time on drug charges.

To deal with these unruly, drug-addicted prisoners, two federal government bureaucrats, the Bureau of Prisons' James V. Bennett and the Public Health Service's Walter Treadway, proposed a compromise. To placate wardens the two lobbied for a bill to establish

On March 19, 1939, *The Denver Post* ran a full-page feature on the Narcotic Farm: "A few scant years ago," wrote C. S. van Dresser, "dope addicts were treated as criminals, and thrown into penitentiaries, jails, and county lock-ups along with burglars, felons and murderers....Today, this inhuman treatment is slated for the discard, for Uncle Sam has come to the decision that drug addicts are not criminals—they are sick people, both mentally and physically—and if given proper understanding and treatment, stand a fair chance of getting on their feet and returning to the world to live normal lives."

This general view shows the immensity of the United States narcotic farm near Lexington, Ky.

Drug Addicts Have a Future

By C. S. van Dresser

Great Narcotic Farm

Operated by United States

Public Health Service Is

Achieving Excellent Results

IT IS estimated by the United States public health service that there are between 100,000 and 125,000 dope addicts in America. To the average person that probably means these people are inevitably slated for an ever-mounting hell on earth, and are destined to die a horrible death compared to which Prometheus of Greek mythology had a picnic. Prometheus, it may be remembered, was chained to a rock while buzzards tore out and devoured his liver every day the liver obligingly grew again overnight.

Maybe you feel sorry for a victim coming out of a narcotic-induced flight into Never-Never Land. You believe he is a creature apart—his mental and physical structures wrecked beyond repair—you think he has retreated into a world apart—afraid to face his fellow man—ashamed beyond description of his weakness, and completely unwilling to look into his future.

Such an individual may be committed to a private or public institution—there to be forgotten as conveniently as possible.

A SCANT few years ago such an attitude on the part of the American public was reasonably justifiable. With but few exceptions, there were no established institutions for the treatment of drug addicts. Dope addicts were treated as criminals, and thrown into penitentiaries, jails and county lock-ups along with burglars, felons and murderers. Every state in the union, along with the federal government, had varying forms of punishment for the illegal use of habit-forming drugs, and addicts, deprived of the stimulus their systems craved, suffered horrible tortures at the hands of law-enforcement officers.

Today, this dreadful treatment is slated for the discard, for Uncle Sam has come to the decision that drug addicts are not criminals—they are sick people—both mentally and physically—and if given proper and understanding treatment, stand a fair chance of getting on their feet and returning to the world to live normal, healthy lives.

To this end, the United States government, thru its public health service, has built and put into operation the most unique hospital of its kind in America, if not the entire world.

The hospital is known as the Narcotic farm and is situated near Lexington, in the rolling, bluegrass country of Kentucky.

Technically, the institution is a prison, to which violators of federal drug laws are committed for varying lengths of time for treatment. In reality, it is far from a prison, for there are no gun-toting guards nor escape-proof walls. Despite this seeming laxity, escape at Lexington is virtually unknown. Indeed, in this respect, the hospital has the best record of any federal institution in the land. As a matter of fact, the inmates of the farm are referred to as a "beneficiaries," and in no theoretical sense of the word are they "prisoners."

The institution, an excerpt from United States government regulations concerning management of the narcotic farm reads as follows: "Prisoners shall not be held to prevent the departure of any honorable beneficiaries." And furthermore: "A guardian shall use only reasonable and necessary physical force as beneficiaries in defense of himself or another person attacked by a beneficiary."

THERE are four types of inmates at Lexington. Most of these are technically termed "prisoners" and have been sentenced by a federal judge to serve a term for their addiction. From these ranks are drawn the second classification, known as "ex-prisoners." Men who voluntarily elect to stay at the farm after their full term has expired in order to continue treatment, fall into this class.

The third type of inmate is designated as a "probationer." He has been put on probation by a federal judge, contingent upon his agreeing to take the cure at Lexington. In such cases, the United States government furnishes

(See Two)

transportation for the addict who, more frequently than not, takes the trip to Lexington without any guardian.

Strangely enough, those who really want to enter the institution have the most difficult time getting there. Most of these, designated as "volunteers" at Lexington, realize the terrific problem they have to face and have a sincere and honest desire for help. However, before being admitted to the cure, their personal records are closely checked because a certain percentage of those have the mistaken idea that Uncle Sam is in the business of supplying free shots of morphine and opium to established dope fiends, who with all their zest for a sniff of "snow." Needless to say, the setup at Lexington is in direct opposition to such a theory.

DURING the period of its inception and throughout the year of its major development, the Narcotic farm has been directed by Dr. Walter L. Treadway, former assistant surgeon of the

Agriculture is one of the methods used in treatment of narcotic addicts and the United States farm at Lexington is well equipped for the purpose. Here are the dairy barns of the institution.

United States public health service. The institution was under the management of Dr. Lawrence Kolb of the service.

"It is amazing," Dr. Treadway states, "how much dope a man's system can absorb. Over a period of years, he can build up a resistance to a terrific amount of opium. Once he has been weaned away from the drug, a mere fraction of the original amount has system had previously been standing would kill him outright."

Continues Dr. Treadway: "We have learned several things at Lexington that I believe are not generally known. Opium and its derivatives—morphine, heroin and codeine—are the only habit-forming drugs in the true medicinal sense of the word. To be more explicit, these drugs set up what is known as a 'physical dependence,' which means that

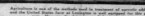

Electric therapy equipment of the latest design is used in the treatment of narcotic addicts. At left is one of the laboratories at the Lexington farm.

every patient is treated as an individual and not as a mere case history."

Previous to addiction the patient has been under a heavy mental strain. He is a young fellow (average age for contraction of the habit is 27), out of a job and worried to death. He takes to drink, and one morning after a wild siege of overindulgence he wakes up with the all-American hangover. A friend suggests an authoritative pickup—the man takes a "shot in the arm" and thus becomes a potential inmate for Lexington.

Odd as it may seem, another facet of the picture is presented by doctors and nurses. Despite the fact that these persons know more than any other the deadly effects of morphine and heroin, having easy access to these drugs results in not a few inmates of Lexington coming from these professional groups.

a man's body demands the narcotic much the same way that a normal person craves meat, bread, milk or other essentials of sustenance.

"Such physical dependence does not hold true with the user of cocaine, marijuana, peyote and other narcotics. Rather it is a case of desired mental stimulus after an emotional let-down—the let-down being caused by a wearing off of the excitement caused by such drugs as the first place."

What is the cure for opium addiction? The answer is that is simple—there is no definite cure. The program at Lexington is too low to permit of a standard, fool-proof formula for the cure of this affliction. As Dr. Treadway puts it: "Each case presents its particular problem. The mind as well as the body is afflicted, and therefore

However, whether the patient be drawn from the social register or the "wrong side of the tracks," he binds at the Narcotic farm, convicted and sentenced by a federal judge for drug addiction. If the doctor in charge, after a painstaking physical examination, are convinced that his system can "take it," he is taken off the drug immediately and no arguments listened to. Admittedly it's a bit tough on the patient, but the doctors work on the well-founded theory that the quickest way is the easiest way for all concerned.

ON THE other hand, if the patient is run down and in bad shape, he is given decreasing doses of codeine until he is gradually tapered off to the zero point in drug consumption.

In either case, the victim goes thru a temporary hell of his own making. After his last "shot" wears off—usually between five and twelve hours—he will begin to get severe cramps and pains in his stomach and muscles; sleep

will be unknown to him for several nights. If he has been using narcotics heavily he will suffer terribly from violent spasms of vomiting and diarrhea. As a rule he will go thru this combination of agonies for about three or four days, the climax being reached around the middle of the second day.

THE easiest part of the job of curing a drug addict is getting his physical system straightened out, says Dr. Treadway. Unlinking the mental quirks that originally led to his downfall is the principal difficulty. To that end each patient is studied individually, and all encouragement possible is given him to pursue any normal interests he may have had before he virtually surrendered to drugs.

For instance: The Narcotic farm boasts a fine library which is patronized by many of the patients. Those musically inclined join the band and concerts of classical and popular music are given regularly.

The Lexington institution is aptly named "farm," for many garden products are grown on the 1,000-acre grounds, the surplus being canned for use during winter months, the patients doing all the work. It might be mentioned here that no manual labor of any kind is compulsory. In addition, the athletic grounds, with its softball and baseball fields, present a scene of manly energy and activity afternoons.

Books and magazines are not censored, and the radio is a most valued medium of information and amusement. Motion pictures are intensely popular, the regular Saturday night shows being topnotch.

WHAT is probably the most astonishing of all is that the patients write, edit and publish their own newspaper. It is called the Thoroughbred, and the first edition came out only a few months ago. Very little supervision is exercised over the journal, which the United States public health service staff has the authority to delete any material considered injurious. There has been very little blue-penciling to date.

In the very first edition the following plea, which gives an idea of the sincerity and longing for normalcy of the inmate resident, is printed by the editor:

"Patients are invited to contribute comments, articles, short stories, poetry and jokes. What may seem trivial to you may appeal to other patients. We are living in a little world of our own, and incidents that might not interest those on the outside are to have here. Also, if you bear a good joke on the floor or some funny bit in a newspaper, jot it down and send it in. We do not all read the same papers nor listen to the same radio programs. Anyway, let us do the best we can. That is all any one could expect."

Is it any wonder, in the face of such a courageous statement, that Dr. Treadway states that a narcotic addict, if given the opportunity, has a fighting chance to resume a healthful, happy life?

Copyright, 1939.

prisons as hospitals where addicts could get medical treatment to cure their addiction. The two convinced Congress that addicts could be rehabilitated, and a bill authorizing the construction of two "narcotics farms" was passed in 1929. Three years later, ground-breaking for the first "US Narcotic Farm" took place in Lexington, Kentucky. In 1935 the institution opened to great fanfare, and in 1938 a second, similar narcotics hospital was completed in Fort Worth, Texas. For decades these institutions would be among the only publicly available drug treatment facilities in the nation.

The US Narcotic Farm became the centerpiece of what was hailed in the press as a "New Deal for the Drug Addict." On opening day Dr. Lawrence Kolb, the institution's first director, held that the Narcotic Farm marked "a new era" in the nation's efforts to control drug addiction. In a statement filmed for national newsreel distribution he declared: "Now addicts will no longer be merely sent to prison for what is really a weakness, but will be given the best medical treatment that science can afford in an atmosphere designed to rehabilitate them spiritually, mentally, and physically." Incarcerated addicts who were sent to the institution would no longer be called "prisoners" but rather "patients," because they were there for treatment and rehabilitation.

Treatment followed the precepts of moral therapy, a popular nineteenth-century approach to treating mental and psychological disorders with discipline and compassion in a healthful, rural setting. Patients were kept busy with vocational therapy, group or individual psychotherapy, religious services, and indoor and outdoor recreation. But labor was the basic organizing principle behind the therapy first offered at the Narcotic Farm when it opened. Patients could work as farmhands, factory workers, tradesmen, or as domestic help in the homes of the prison staff. Working at Narco, recovering narcotics addicts could acquire skills to be auto mechanics, carpenters, electricians, barbers, draftsmen, cobblers, dental hygienists, printers, and even musical instrument repairmen.

Recreation was also promoted as healthy and morally therapeutic for the addicts there, all of whom were encouraged to live by social norms embraced by mainstream society. From Lexington's earliest days there were tennis and basketball courts, bowling alleys, boxing rings, billiard and ping-pong tables, and even a golf course, all of which earned the institution a reputation as a "country-club prison." For those who preferred activities other than sports there were arts and crafts, basket weaving, painting, and an extensive library. But the one form of recreational therapy that made Narco famous was music. Over the years, hundreds of musicians, many of them incarcerated on narcotics charges, took part in the institution's open-air concerts, dances, and Friday-night shows for the inmates and public.

After World War II, when opiate embargoes were lifted and shipping routes restored, organized crime picked up where it had left off before the war, importing large quantities of heroin into urban America. By 1949 the nation's first youth heroin epidemic was under way. David Deitch, a Narco patient in 1951, recalls this new population of addicts as minorities and whites from the underclass, drawn to urban centers to find opportunity. Yet this population, often disillusioned by racism and the lack of opportunity they encountered upon arriving in cities, saw an explosion of drug use among its young. Heroin use caught on with the teenage children of Irish, Italian, and Jewish immigrants, as well as with young Puerto Ricans and African Americans.

This new cohort of addicts was anathema to law enforcement and, in 1951, Federal Bureau of Narcotics chief Harry J. Anslinger energetically endorsed two-year mandatory minimum sentences for first-time possession of narcotics convictions. Congress passed this law, as well as the draconian Narcotics Control Act of 1956, which called for five-year minimum sentences for first-time possession and included a death penalty provision for dealers. The sum effect of these laws—which doctors at Narco publicly opposed—was that younger and younger people were going away for longer and longer periods of time. A typical case study from Narco's files follows:

> At nineteen he began to use heroin, and shortly thereafter was placed on probation for three years for forging a narcotics prescription. After one year he violated probation by returning to the use of narcotic drugs. He was committed to Lexington for four years, was granted parole after serving more than two years, and was returned after a few months as a violator. He had again relapsed. He was again committed to Lexington. Three months after his conditional release in the summer of 1957, he was again using drugs and a few weeks later was returned to custody as a violator.

By the late 1950s the institution was feeling the strain of a population of young addicts embittered by long sentences. Many turned increasingly resentful of and unwilling to go along with the institution's old-fashioned notions of moral therapy and self-improvement. Disciplinary reports among this increasingly young population of inmates were up, and many who came there for treatment left the place knowing more about drugs than they knew coming in. Here, patients learned from each other how to get by during drug

This photo appeared in a 1951 *New York World-Telegram and Sun* series on the prison. The original caption read: "This desperate narcotics addict, caught like his fellows in the revolving door of law enforcement, will probably go back to his habit when he is free." Photo by Robert E. Stigers.

shortages, where to cop when they got home, which local doctors to manipulate for drugs, who were informants, and who were reliable connections. Narco had become a fraternity for drug addicts, a center of junkie culture revealed to a curious public by William S. Burroughs and other authors who passed through its wards. Twenty-five years into Narco's elusive quest to "cure" addiction, one of its founders wrote, presciently: "The problem seems well on its way to once again becoming a 'prison problem.' I confess we face this prospect with a feeling of discouragement and a sense of futility."

The New Deal Is Put Out to Pasture

In 1966, President Lyndon B. Johnson signed legislation known as the Narcotic Addict Rehabilitation Act, or NARA. This legislation changed Narco in fundamental ways. It would no longer be a prison but rather a treatment hospital for addicts facing drug-related charges, all of whom could avoid prison time by volunteering to go to Lexington for "the cure."

With the federal government recognizing that the old cure had failed, a new treatment staff was brought in, and novel, experimental treatment practices were instituted. By 1968 the agricultural operation was shut down, and instead of using farmwork and other vocations for occupational therapy, patients were organized into therapeutic "houses" that used peer pressure to bring about a change in drug-taking behavior. Prison bars were removed; the walls were painted bright, fresh colors; the front gates were unlocked; and group therapy started taking place outside in the fresh air.

But NARA would prove to be a disappointment as the relapse rate, which hovered around 90 percent throughout the life of the institution, remained unchanged. In 1974 Narco was closed as a therapeutic center and subsequently taken over by the Bureau of Prisons. Now surrounded by cyclone fences and razor wire, today the institution belies little of its founding ideals as a humane treatment center for drug addicts. Declared a Federal Medical Center in the early 1990s, the former Narcotic Farm now provides health care to seriously ill federal prisoners.

The Science of a Social Problem

Within its walls, the Narcotic Farm housed a discrete laboratory dedicated to finding answers to the most fundamental questions about addiction: Why do some drug users become addicted while others do not? What makes addicts willing to sacrifice home, family, and everything they care about for a substance that is obviously killing them? What causes relapse? For decades the Addiction Research Center at Narco was the only lab in the world devoted solely to this scientific quest.

When the Narcotic Farm opened in 1935, drug addiction was an obscure topic within medicine. Most doctors knew nothing about it.

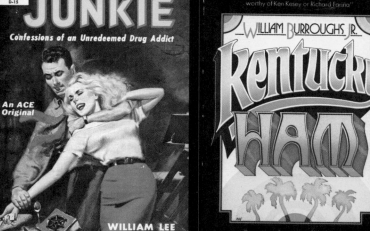

TWO BOOKS IN ONE   35c

ACE
DOUBLE
BOOKS
D-15

JUNKIE
Confessions of an Unredeemed Drug Addict

An ACE
Original

WILLIAM LEE

D2658 • $1.50 • A BERKLEY MEDALLION BOOK

"A comic journey through hell...
worthy of Ken Kesey or Richard Farina"

WILLIAM BURROUGHS, JR.
Kentucky HAM

"...a marvelous sense of black humor
...a writer with a distinctive and effective voice
that one hopes will be heard more." *Rolling Stone*

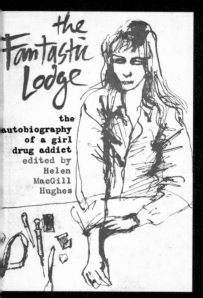

the Fantastic Lodge

the autobiography of a girl drug addict

edited by
Helen
MacGill
Hughes

AWARD BOOK Ⓐ A659S 75¢ MAC

"HAUNTINGLY BEAUTIFUL NOVEL
LACED WITH OBSCENITY...
UNUSUAL, FASCINATING..."
—FORT WORTH STAR-TELEGRAM

"WRITTEN IN GUT-LEVEL
LANGUAGE...COMPELLING"
—LIBRARY JOURNAL

"POWERFUL"—CLEVELAND PRESS

THE FARM

but the hope that science had the power to solve this problem prompted Congress to call for an ambitious research program at Narco that would study the disease and find a cure for those who suffered from it. To achieve these goals researchers at Lexington would need to study addicts themselves. They set out to do so by re-addicting a handful of federal inmates to morphine in order to study changes that occurred as they went through the entire addiction cycle of intoxication, dependence, and withdrawal.

Ethical questions arose immediately. Narco's first director, Dr. Lawrence Kolb, rationalized the practice of experimental re-addiction on grounds that researchers would only use "hopeless addicts" who would inevitably relapse anyway. His Public Health Service counter-parts were concerned that prisoners could not freely volunteer for research because the prison environment was inherently coercive. The inherent contradiction of re-addicting people in need of rehabili-tation and the impossibility of truly "voluntary" participation in prison research foreshadowed national ethics investigations, which would end the institution's human research forty years later.

Despite these early ethical concerns, Narco's congressional man-date to find a scientific cure for addiction and the need to justify the research unit's existence with scientific results were powerful motiva-tors to continue research. The program began in a separate lab inside the institution with a small, full-time staff including a biochemist, pharmacologist, physiologist, psychiatrist, psychologist, lab techni-cian, and four guards. They began with a yearlong study of six former morphine addicts who had volunteered to be test subjects. Four inmates were given morphine and carefully studied both physically and psychologically. The other two served as a control group and would not receive drugs.

The general research design established in this first study contin-ued fundamentally unchanged for the next four decades of scien-tific inquiry at Lexington. Incarcerated former heroin and morphine addicts, most serving long sentences, would volunteer for studies ranging from single-dose morphine tests to months-long LSD studies to yearlong experiments with habit-forming pharmaceuticals such as barbiturates. No one died as a result of being in any tests and involvement in research was seen as desirable by many inmates, in part because participants got time off their sentences, or, up until 1955, payment in drugs. After completing the tests, all were given Narco's standard six months of rehabilitation to ensure that they were no longer physically dependent when they were discharged from the institution.

The practice of using addicts for research quickly gained momen-tum at Lexington, and for most of its history almost no one within the

22

This photograph shows early research at Narco. The apparatus in the center of the photo was designed to test the mental reactions of those under the influence of morphine. The "patient" on the right is an actor posing for promotional material created by the government to publicize the Narcotic Farm. Photo by Arthur Rothstein, 1939.

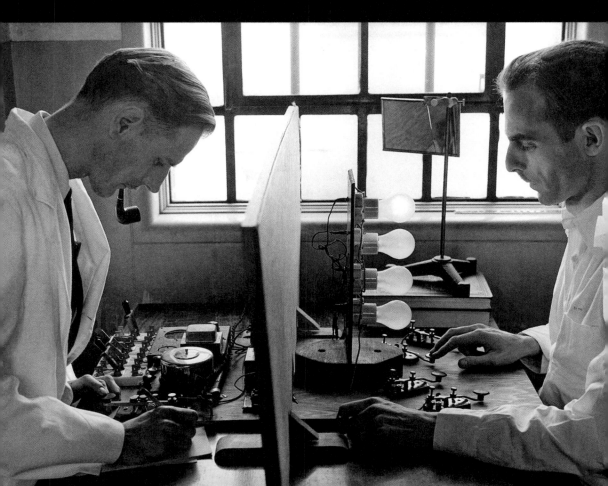

institution questioned it. Unique access to human subjects garnered the Addiction Research Center, as Narco's research lab was called, a celebrated position in medicine. While it might seem surprising today, medical research on prisoners was both legal and common in America in the 1930s through the 1960s, and the ARC's practices, publicized in newspapers, magazines, top-flight scientific journals, and on television, went virtually unquestioned by the general public.

Not surprisingly, researchers in the ARC rarely wanted for experimental subjects. There was always a long waiting list to get into the program, and once in, many inmates volunteered again and again. Within the lab, researchers and addicts both got what they wanted: Researchers gained insights in their quest to find a "cure" for addiction, and addicts got the drugs that they craved. Former Lexington patient Bernie Kolb worked as a typist in the ARC and remembers that "the guys on research just had a great life; they'd sit around, play cards, nod in the corner. I mean, hey, would you rather wait around for some kind of dope to be shot into you or work on the farm?"

The patients were fascinating to the half dozen Public Health Service doctors working in the ARC. As in the larger institution, drugs were the preferred topic of conversation. Many addicts were highly articulate and sophisticated about which drugs they liked and why. Some went into detail about their lives before incarceration: where they came from, what their families were like, how they got addicted. These stories were of keen interest to researchers, because they informed a deeper understanding of the cultural, sociological, and psychological factors found within what was, at the time, a little-known population of "dope fiends."

Some of the lab's earliest work investigated commonly held beliefs about these dope fiends, including the notions that addicts could be spotted by telltale physical characteristics or that they had subaverage intelligence. Both long-held assumptions proved false. Another task was demonstrating that none of the many medicines marketed as "cures" for addiction did anything to ease withdrawal or "cure" addicts. Once it had dispelled these bogus medical theories, the ARC set about almost single-handedly creating the knowledge base of understanding on which the modern science of addiction was built.

The ARC doctors believed that morphine, the archetypal addictive opiate, held the key to unlocking the mysteries of all addiction. In their quest to understand, researchers carefully studied every aspect of morphine's interaction with man, developing the first quantitative scales for measuring degrees of addiction, severity of withdrawal, and the addictiveness of other drugs. This knowledge yielded deeper understanding of addiction, but it couldn't explain why addicts who had been clean for years at Narco were unable to resist the lure of

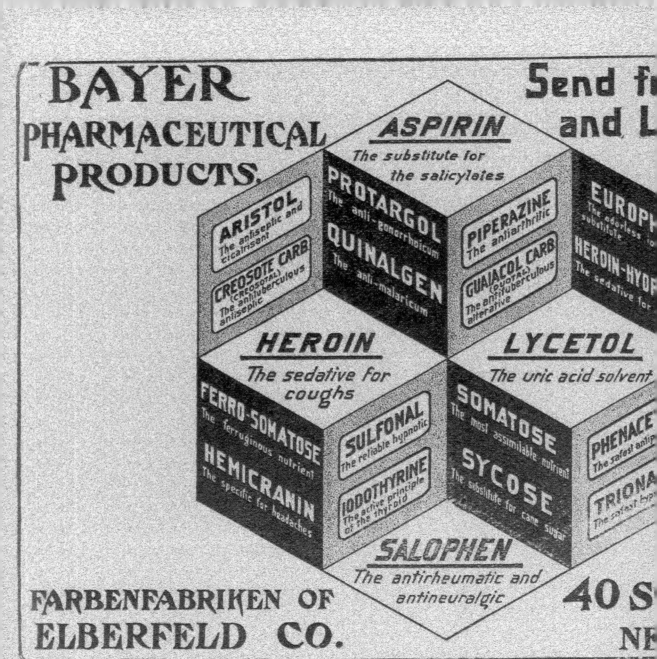

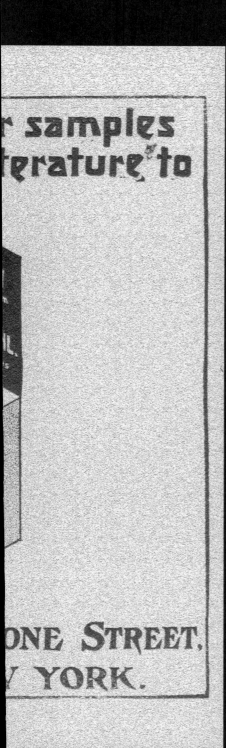

icked the symptoms of actual withdrawal as they neared their home cities for the first time.

This problem of relapse vexed the ARC doctors, especially Dr. Abe Wikler, a psychiatrist influenced by the behavioral theories of Ivan Pavlov. He was intrigued by inmates' stories of sudden, irresistible cravings and began to suspect that relapse resulted in part from a conditioned response to cues in an addict's environment. Wikler reasoned that patients were returning to neighborhoods where every person and every object was associated with the experience of hustling for, scoring, and then using drugs. Like the sound of a ringing bell triggering hunger in Pavlov's dogs, these subconscious associations could trigger both a psychological desire and a physical craving for dope. Today this language of cues and triggers is ubiquitous in drug treatment, is accepted as fundamental to the recurring nature of the disease, and remains one of the ARC's greatest contributions to the understanding of addiction and relapse.

As the lab made discovery after discovery in its new field, it became the acknowledged international center for addiction science and eventually published more than 500 articles in leading medical and psychiatric journals. It was also uniquely qualified for another project important to public health: For most of the lab's history, the ARC was the key player in a US government program to evaluate the addiction potential of new pharmaceuticals so that addictive drugs could be kept off the market or legally controlled. The list of pharmaceuticals tested includes many still in use: buprenorphine, clonidine, codeine, cyclazocine, Darvon, Demerol, Dilaudid, amphetamines, ketobemidone, Thorazine, tranquilizers such as Miltown, and barbiturates used as sedatives and sleeping pills.

For the ARC, testing these drugs was not just a matter of scientific inquiry or performing a valuable service to the pharmaceutical industry. The ARC saw itself as safeguarding public health on a global scale by preventing addictive compounds from destroying the lives of thousands. Heroin was the specter that kept the ARC committed to pre- market testing in an era before clinical trials were required by the FDA. Initially heralded as a "wonder drug" when the Bayer company released it as a potent cough medicine in 1898, heroin had been considered "nonaddictive" in the days before much was known about addiction.

The drug-testing protocol proceeded as follows: The first test was whether former addicts liked a new drug; if they got high—and many did—the drug was recommended for further study. Researchers then turned to subjects who had been re-addicted to morphine and then plunged into the excruciating throes of cold-turkey withdrawal. If the experimental drug alleviated their withdrawal symptoms, then the new drug was considered a good substitute for morphine and very likely highly addictive. Over the decades, hundreds of opiate addicts in tests like these would experience everything from euphoria to intense suffering as part of the lab's quest to unmask dangerously addictive pharmaceuticals.

One example of a dangerous substance that the ARC succeeded in keeping from the American public was ketobemidone, a drug still used today as a potent analgesic for postoperative pain and cancer pain. Convinced by test results that this synthetic opiate was as addictive as morphine, the ARC recommended stringent controls, which were placed on American production and sales in 1954. Though relatively unknown in the United States, the drug caused, as the ARC suspected it would, a significant abuse problem in countries where it was less strictly controlled. The ARC's public health victory against the dangers of ketobemidone was often cited by Harris Isbell, the lab's director from 1945 to 1962, as one of its most significant accomplishments.

The researchers' "holy grail" was to find a drug with all the painkilling properties of morphine and none of its addictive qualities—but they never found it. That quest remains a dream despite nearly a century of attempts. But one new synthetic opiate the lab tested on humans—methadone—would go on to have a long and controversial history. The ARC pioneered the use of methadone in addiction treatment, establishing safe therapeutic dosage levels so that it could be used in detoxifying opiate addicts. It was the first significant aid to opiate withdrawal, and although it was not a "cure" for addiction, methadone offered hope that a pharmacologic "cure" for addiction could some day be found.

The ARC was the only place in the world where abuse potential was assessed in human beings. As a result, the US government, foreign governments, the United Nations, and the World Health Organization all depended on it for data and predictions of which drugs posed potential public health problems. Within the United States, the ARC handled this task well into the 1970s, when controversy about its use of incarcerated test subjects brought the research program to a point of ethical crisis.

Prisoners' rights movements in the early seventies led public opinion to grow increasingly critical of prison research. According to the emerging view of the time, which holds today, prisoners are vulnerable to exploitative research practices because the harshness of prison conditions may lead them to participate in tests they would not submit to if they were not incarcerated. The ARC's scientists, long accustomed to conducting research without public scrutiny, found themselves on the defensive when, in 1972, it was revealed that Public Health Service researchers in Tuskegee, Alabama, had continued a study of untreated syphilis in African-American men long after an effective treatment was available. This deeply unsettling news tainted many PHS projects, including the work of the ARC. The ARC researchers defended their practice of using inmates as volunteers for their drug research, saying, in part, that all research subjects had a clear idea of the work that was being done and could withdraw from any experiment if they found it unpleasant. This defense held little sway with a general public that was increasingly skeptical about the ethics of government science and government scientists themselves. But the scandal that ultimately tainted the ARC's reputation can be summed up in just six letters: CIA, LSD.

From 1953 to 1962 the ARC's director, Harris Isbell, had accepted CIA money for LSD research and had recruited inmates to participate in all varieties of LSD studies. As would later be known following the discovery of CIA documents, throughout the Cold War the American military and intelligence community was interested in using LSD as an interrogation tool and as an incapacitating agent. Over the course of a decade, millions of dollars were given to the ARC as part of a nationwide, but covert drug program known as MK-ULTRA. Much of the CIA-funded, MK-ULTRA drug research can only be described as an American tragedy—it was unethical, unscientific, and often conducted on unwitting subjects, at least one of whom died as a result of bad science. But contrasted to the famously reckless "experiments" carried out by CIA operative George Hunter White, as well as those conducted by researchers on military bases and universities, the ARC did careful and meticulous studies, many of which were published in major medical journals and are still considered valid—even groundbreaking—research on LSD today.

In a 1975 congressional hearing on human experimentation and the MK-ULTRA program, former ARC director Harris Isbell groped for words to explain the research program to which he had devoted his life. He allowed as to how the "ethical codes were not so well developed" in the 1950s, but he also defended the ARC's practices, saying that the inmates had volunteered for the tests after being informed of what was going to happen to them.

Public exposure ended business as usual at the ARC. In the charged political climate of the seventies, prisoners were judged incapable of giving informed consent behind federal bars. No longer would American society consider it ethical to re-addict imprisoned addicts for the sake of science, and on December 31, 1976, the last human test subject was transferred out of the laboratory. Never again would addiction research be a centralized enterprise. From then until the present day, it has taken place in a far-flung constellation of centers and research groups employing a variety of approaches, among them human drug testing on addicts who volunteer off the street. In the end the ARC was packed up and moved to Baltimore, Maryland, where it became the intramural research program of the National Institute on Drug Abuse (NIDA).

The Addiction Research Center's legacy is that it established an entire scientific field and formulated the current definition of addiction as a chronic, relapsing brain disorder. It also trained a cadre of addiction specialists who themselves went on to work as heads of medical schools, government officials, directors of drug treatment centers, and leaders in addiction research.

Today, addiction remains a scientific and clinical puzzle. Yet despite addiction taking its place as a scientific problem, the courts continue to send drug addicts to prisons where they cannot get treatment. A new impossible dream grips the public imagination—that the United States will become a "drug-free" nation. Perhaps the day will come when more sensible views prevail—that relapse is the norm; that drug addiction should be treated as a chronic, relapsing problem that affects the public health; and that meeting people's basic needs will dampen their enthusiasm for drugs. Until then, effective drug policy will prove as elusive a quest as the impossible dreams that built the Narcotic Farm.

a patient's head to measure eye movements as part of a barbiturate test. Photo by Bill Strode, 1966.

About the Photographs

This collection of photographs emerged from research undertaken by JP Olsen and Luke Walden for a documentary film on the Narcotic Farm, and by Dr. Nancy D. Campbell for a book on the history of addiction research in the United States. Between us we conducted dozens of interviews with former Narco staff, volunteer patients, and inmates, and along the way heard many tales of "the box that got away," of lost research films, and photos and ephemera that no one bothered to keep. But we also discovered rare film footage, countless documents, dozens of journalistic accounts of the institution, and more than 2,000 photographs in public and private archives across the country.

The photographs in this book represent a wide range of points of view and evolving social attitudes toward the institution and its mission over the course of its forty-year history. Those photos taken by government employees emphasize the architectural grandeur of the building, its bucolic setting, and the institution's compassionate staff. Some explicitly promote the hospital's aspirations and good work, such as the elegant, staged portrayals of the drug treatment process taken by Farm Security Administration photographer Arthur Rothstein, who travelled to the Narcotic Farm on assignment in 1939. Other photos, produced by the institution's staff, include 35mm Kodachrome snapshots that proudly document the farming operation and depict inmates working industriously to ready themselves for conventional life outside the institution.

News photographs from the 1950s reveal the era's prevailing public attitude of disdain for "dope fiends." Lurid, flash-lit press camera photos from national dailies and magazines portray Lexington's addicts as abject spectacles of moral degradation, their faces averted in apparent shame. In these stories addiction is depicted as sin, withdrawal as torture, and rehabilitation an impossible dream.

In the 1960s, photojournalists using 35mm cameras and high-speed film told the story of Lexington with a new visual approach and a more sympathetic sensibility that reflected changing public attitudes toward addicts. Pulitzer Prize-winning photographer Bill Strode and *Life* magazine's Bill Eppridge capture the inmate point of view, peering through layers of prison bars and using available light and wide angle lenses to communicate the human experience of Narco's overwhelming physical scale. In candid, compositionally beautiful photos we see patients going about their daily lives—playing tennis, performing jazz, undergoing psychotherapy, or submitting to voluntary re-addiction in the research lab—as shadowy, anonymous figures subsumed in a total institution.

The photographs in this book have never before been collected in one place. Together they tell a story of noble aspirations and a time when American science and ingenuity were thought capable of solving any problem, even drug addiction. This archive preserves the memory of this grand experiment.

A cow's-eye view of the Narcotic Farm's facade in its pastoral setting.

An aerial photograph from the early 1950s shows the Narcotic Farm's 1,000 acres. In the foreground is Kolb Hall, built in 1941 to house female patients; to the right are the farm's barns and silos. A small community of homes for high-ranking officers and their families is nestled to the right of the water tower.

01

A New Deal for the Drug Addict

The Narcotic Farm's dual roles as prison and hospital reflected

a long-standing American ambivalence about addiction. Should drug addicts be punished as criminals? Or should they be treated as people with an illness?

Both views—still contested today—strongly influenced Narco's design. It was a prison built to confine violators of federal drug laws, but its rural setting and architectural style reflected a rehabilitation philosophy known as moral therapy, commonly associated with hospitals and sanitoriums. Moral therapy held that spending time in a wholesome, rural setting could cure both immoral behavior and also bad health. In the case of the Narcotic Farm, addicts—believed to be sick in both body and will—would regain physical and spiritual health through a regimen of good food, clean air, and hard work. The institution's expectation was that its patients would return to society as decent and productive citizens.

Lexington, Kentucky's temperate climate, fertile soil, and picturesque location were key factors in its selection as the site for the first Narcotic Farm. Groundbreaking began in 1932. Three years and four million dollars later the massive building—which covered twelve acres—stood ready to confine and rehabilitate up to 1,500 inmates.

The institution's size, towering walls, and barred windows powerfully communicated its mission of incarceration. Narco, as the institution was known locally, had a layout typical of other prisons of the time, but its sheer mass was unusual. As former patient Eddie Flowers remembered, "I had been in other prisons—Rikers Island, Sing Sing—but the size of that place really made my jaw drop."

Despite the institution's overbearing scale, therapeutic ideas were central to its design, which included a spacious chapel and a complex grid of courtyards allowing for light and ventilation throughout the institution. Patients' day-rooms were airy sanctuaries where enormous windows gave expansive views of the rural landscape, while the hope for spiritual rehabilitation was symbolized by vaulted ceilings and arched doorways reminiscent of a monastery.

Narco's specialized facilities were meant to manifest the therapeutic potential of medicine, spirituality, and labor. The institution's auto shop and sewing room, with their towering Romanesque window arches, appear in photographs as luminous cathedrals of occupational therapy. Recreational facilities—intended to instill values of sportsmanship and fair play—included tennis courts, a softball diamond, a gymnasium, and a bowling alley. Well-equipped medical, surgical, and dental suites affirmed Narco's commitment to help a diseased population.

The idealistic goal of rehabilitating the nation's drug addicts captured the public imagination, and Narco's opening made front-page news. There was even a local newspaper contest to name the new institution.

Enthusiastic readers suggested names such as Beneficial Farm, Courageous Hospital, and the US Greatest Gift to Lift Mankind Sanatorium. More fanciful entries included Dream Castle, Big Shot Drug Farm, and Alpha Government Home. In the end the government chose a name whose agricultural associations inscribed the ideals of moral therapy in the very walls of the institution. Over the main entrance, carved in stone, the institution bore the words, "United States Narcotic Farm."

The Narcotic Farm / A New Deal for the Drug Addict

The US Narcotic Farm was built under the supervision of the US Treasury Department, which was responsible for the design of federal buildings across the country. The cornerstone, laid in a ceremony in the summer of 1933, lists James A. Wetmore as acting supervising architect. Lafayette Studios, Lexington, Kentucky, ca. 1933.

The US Narcotic Farm opened to fanfare in a ceremony held on May 25, 1935. US Surgeon General Hugh S. Cumming dedicated the institution to "those instinctive demands ever present in the American people that the sick and afflicted shall be set in the way of strength and hope." Lafayette Studios, Lexington, Kentucky, 1935.

The building's physical environment was intended to inspire and reinforce the tenets of "moral therapy." Cloisterlike walkways gave the institution a monastic air, and the farm and dairy barns—central to the institution's ideal of rural rehabilitation—are visible in the background. Photo by Arthur Rothstein, 1939.

The main entry to the institution featured a lofty groin-vaulted ceiling with Art Deco columns and light fixtures. The interior architectural style of the building was, in general, more like a hospital than a prison. Photo by Arthur Rothstein, 1939.

Narco's dental suite. Poor hygiene and malnutrition—hallmarks of long-term heroin addiction—left many addicts with rotting teeth. Dental care was the most common medical treatment performed at Narco; in 1937 the institution logged 21,717 dental treatments and extracted 4,245 teeth. 1935.

Banner headlines proclaimed the US Narcotic Farm to be the dawning of a new era of social progress in which drug addicts would be rehabilitated and drug addiction eradicated. *Atlanta Georgian*, 1935.

MARCH 4, 1935

ATLANTA GEORGIAN

The Light of a New Day

With the federal government opening its two first farms for the cure of narcotic victims, historic progress is recorded in the humanitarian treatment of a serious problem.

This movement should be carried rapidly on. There should be a narcotic-cure farm in every state of the Union.

It is a deplorable fact that ONLY A FEW of the states have adopted the Uniform State Narcotic Law, which is necessary to build up the nation's defenses against the "dope" evil.

Numerous legislatures are now in session. In each of the laggard states IMMEDIATE enactment of the Uniform State Narcotic Law should be compelled by local public opinion.

Failure to adopt the measure will be inexcusable.

02

Competent and Humane

On May 29, 1935, the Narcotic Farm's first federal prisoners
arrived at the institution. Transferred from Leavenworth, Kansas,
the new recruits arrived at a prison unlike any they had ever encountered, one where the staff of doctors, nurses, and medical attendants
outnumbered guards. Guards and doctors alike had been hired with
the understanding that they would accept the notion that drug addicts
deserved humane treatment. Dr. Lawrence Kolb, the institution's
first director, recruited his staff—described in a promotional film as
"competent and humane"—from among the best the US Public
Health Service had to offer.

At a time when narcotics addiction treatment was in its infancy,
Kolb and his team set about designing a rehabilitation program based
on the idea that most addicts had personality disorders that could be
adjusted through job training, psychiatric analysis, and talk therapy.
To engender doctor and patient trust—and to educate doctors on the
disease of addiction—Kolb established a psychiatry residency, one of
the nation's first, where young doctors rotated through the prison on
two-year government contracts. Most of these psychiatric residents
sought housing in nearby Lexington. But in some cases they took
up shelter in the institution itself. Dr. Conan Kornetsky, a psychology
graduate student at the University of Kentucky who worked in the
research lab from 1948 to 1952, recalls: "I had a room with bars on it
just like the prisoner patients, but I had a key so I could come and go."

Such unusual living arrangements were one of the institution's many
quirks. The institution was set up much like a military barracks, with
high-ranking officials given free government housing on its grounds.
Kolb and subsequent directors occupied a grand Georgian-style
mansion. Other employees raised children in a cluster of small homes
that stood less than 1,000 yards from the prison. The community of
government researchers recall the place as isolated but friendly, a
genteel country environment where government-employed neighbors
played bridge and barbecued together.

The children who grew up there called themselves "Narco Brats."
To many, the 1,000-acre farm was an idyllic place to grow up. Few
of the younger children were aware that their families' cooks, house-
keepers, gardeners, and even babysitters were convicted drug addicts
who had been chosen to work in their homes. "It was a strange,
looking-glass world," explains former Narco Brat Marjorie Senechal.
"There were pigs and cows and kittens in the barn, so there was this
feeling that you lived on this vast farm. And then there were all these
really, really nice people there who . . . I didn't realize when I was
really little that they were all prisoners. But I was happy out there with
my addict friends and horses."

The Narcotic Farm was staffed by commissioned officers from the US Public Health Service, pictured here sporting the traditional maritime uniforms of the PHS. Initially established to quell outbreaks of infectious disease in port cities and give medical care to indigent sailors, the PHS evolved into an agency charged with safeguarding the health of the nation's disenfranchised.

Throughout the first half of the twentieth century the PHS was the treatment of last resort for the nation's outcasts: Lepers, shell-shocked veterans, and destitute sailors all found care and shelter in PHS hospitals. When the government sought to solve addiction through medical treatment, addicts were welcomed into the PHS fold at the Narcotic Farm. 1939.

During the 1930s only ten nurses staffed the hospital and cared for upwards of 1,000 patients. 1939.

58

One of the staff homes on the prison grounds. It was occupied for decades by the farm's administrator, Robert Maclin, and his family. 1933.

This Georgian-style mansion housed
Narco's first Medical Officer in Charge.

03

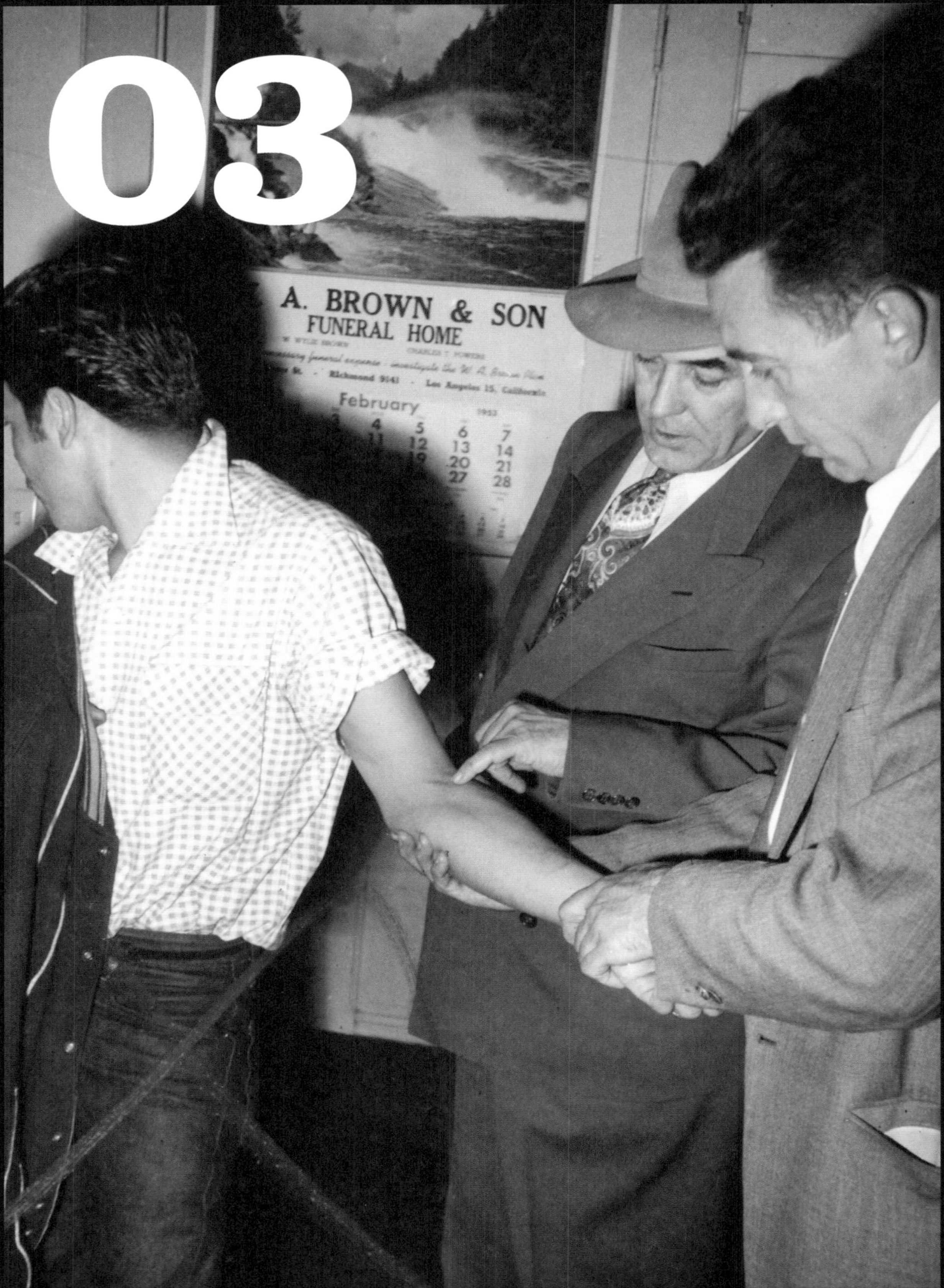
A. BROWN & SON
FUNERAL HOME
Richmond 9141
Los Angeles 15, California
February

The Two Roads to Narco

Over the course of forty years, tens of thousands of men and women were sent to the Narcotic Farm for rehabilitation. Two-thirds of Narco's population had been convicted of violating strict federal drug laws.

The other one-third were "volunteers" who had signed themselves in for treatment. While volunteers could leave anytime, inmates could not. Inside the institution, little distinction was made between the two populations. All patients wore the same clothes, worked the same jobs, ate the same food, enjoyed the same leisure-time activities, and lived together behind bars.

Many of the so-called volunteers turned up at the institution not because they actually wanted to get clean, but because junkie life had simply beaten them down. According to sociologist John Ball, who worked at the institution and studied its addict populations: "You don't go to Lexington when you're running on the street and shooting dope and everything's going fine. It's when your connection is broken, when you've run out of money, the police are after you, and it's time to get out of town."

Those who could afford "the cure" were required to pay a nominal daily fee for the privilege of going to prison. But no one was rejected for lack of funds. However, overcrowding in the 1950s—brought on by a post–World War II teenage heroin epidemic, as well as increasingly harsh drug laws—forced Narco to turn away those who were deemed poor rehabilitation prospects. In many cases, older addicts with a long history of drug use were rejected for treatment to allow room for younger addicts who were believed to stand a better chance of rehabilitation.

Nearly 3,000 voluntary patients came to
the institution each year seeking "the cure."
Photo by Douglas Jones, 1953.

Top: The original *New York World-Telegram and Sun* caption reads: "Two New Jersey state police kick in the front door of a three story frame house in Asbury Park during a pre-dawn crack-down of suspected dope dens in resort area. A dozen were arrested in the Negro area of town." November 15, 1952.

Bottom: The original caption from the *New York World-Telegram and Sun* reads: "Men caught in raids by Federal Agents leave prisoners' van at US Court House in Foley Square today. Forty-five persons were picked up in the opening phase of a nationwide drive to break up a network of drug rings." Photo by Fred Palumbo, January 4, 1952.

65

The original *New York World-Telegram and Sun* caption reads: "Out of the paddy wagons and into the Police Headquarters go some of the 88 dope addicts and pushers rounded up last night in biggest mass drive against narcotics in the city's history. They came from all over the city except Staten Island and in their possession cocaine, heroin, marijuana." Photo by Ed Ford, November 12, 1955.

67

Eight men declare themselves drug addicts before a Lexington judge in order to be sent to Narco to receive the six-month "cure." The original caption from this photograph reads: "Several times a week, the scene shown here is repeated in one of the courts... Like most groups of addicts, this group contains men from several cities who came here to seek help." The men in this photo come from New York, Chicago, Philadelphia, and Richmond, Virginia. 1951.

A volunteer patient is checked into the
Admissions Unit by security staff member
Herbert Sledd. Photo by Douglas Jones, 1953.

Many volunteers simply showed up at the main gate and declared themselves drug addicts in hopes of gaining admission. Photo by Douglas Jones, 1953.

The original caption for this photo, which appeared in the *Lexington Herald*, stated that the two women shown "looked and felt trapped today when it developed that they couldn't get into the US Public Health Service Hospital to take the cure for morphine addiction." 1951.

During the 1950s increasingly punitive drug laws and rising heroin use among teens filled the institution to near capacity. Many volunteers, particularly older addicts considered poor rehabilitation prospects, were denied entry. The original caption for this *Lexington Herald* photograph stated that this man "sits on a curb in front of the gate of the US Public Health Service Hospital yesterday afternoon after he was refused admittance. [He] had again confessed to narcotics addiction and his year's sentence was probated provided he enter the hospital. The hospital said he was ineligible for treatment. [He] walked away from the institution—and waited for a ride to town. He spent last night at the Salvation Army, where he went with the help of Travelers Aid." 1953.

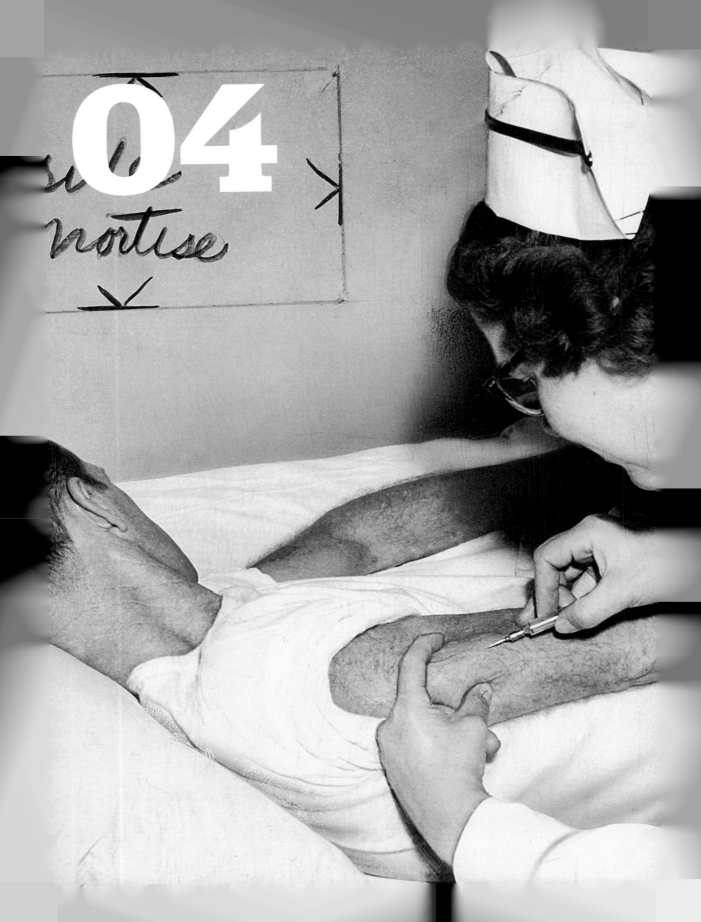

The Lexington Cure

Narco's admission process was similar to that of any federal prison. Upon arrival, convicts and volunteers were photographed, issued a number, and strip-searched. Their shoe soles and boot heels were pried open by security staff vigilantly searching for dope. If any needles or dope were discovered—volunteers frequently arrived stoned and transporting paraphernalia—they were confiscated. Patients were then handed hospital pajamas and sent to the medical ward for a complete physical.

As part of the admission process, volunteers and inmates were compelled to fill out government forms detailing their complete history of drug use: How old were you when you started? What is your drug of choice? How big is your habit? How many times have you tried to quit? Afterward, patients underwent psychological tests designed to assess the severity of their addiction. Barring acute medical emergencies, volunteers were then sent to the detoxification ward (federal convicts were typically already drug-free when they were transported to the institution). On the detox ward, nurses administered morphine shots of gradually decreasing dosages for a safe withdrawal. After 1948, methadone, which was first experimentally tested on inmates inside the institution, was substituted for morphine.

Throughout the institution's forty-year history, the detox process remained essentially unchanged. Usually, upwards of a dozen people were detoxified at one time—men and women were detoxed separately. Former patients recall that nurses doled out barbiturates, known as "goofballs," to blunt the effects of opiate withdrawal. Patients were also treated with "flow baths"—essentially a primitive Jacuzzi—to help soothe their frayed nerves.

Patients' recollections of detox vary. John Stallone, who had kicked drugs numerous times before, remembers the Lexington cure as very pleasant. To author William S. Burroughs, however, who showed up in the late 1940s and recounted his experience in the semi-autobiographical novel *Junkie*, detox at Narco merely delayed and "suspended the sickness" of heroin withdrawal. Yet Burroughs was likely in the minority. Most addicts preferred detoxing at Lexington to going "cold turkey" in city and country jails where, reputation had it, lawmen harassed and sometimes savagely beat those who complained about their suffering.

In all, detoxification lasted slightly less than two weeks. Patients were then sent into the general prison population so rehabilitation could begin.

A patient undergoes an X-ray examination as part of a full medical workup given to patients upon arrival. Many patients came to Narco with preexisting and often painful conditions, including cancer and tuberculosis. Much of Narco's population had little access to health care since hospitals frequently refused to treat addicts. For many, there was quite literally nowhere else to go. Photo by Arthur Rothstein, 1939.

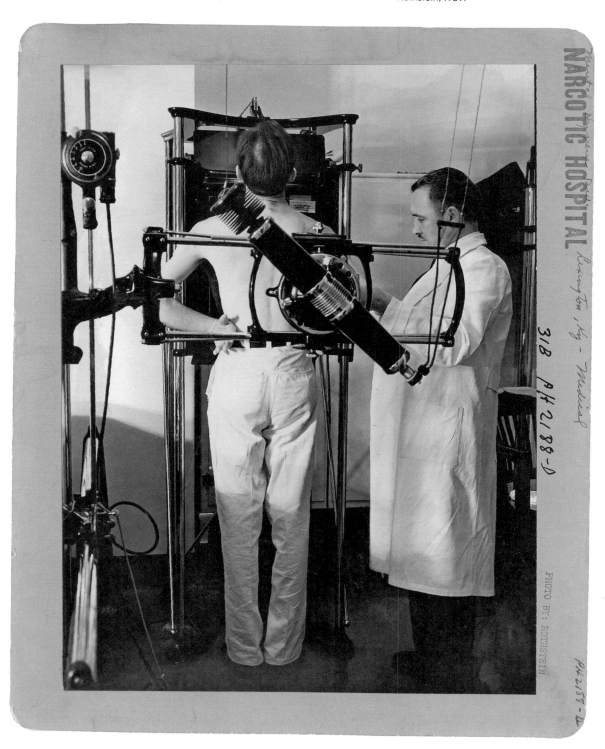

"Works" confiscated during admissions. The bent spoon was used to heat heroin for use in injecting the drug with a hypodermic syringe, here wrapped in paper. Photo by Arthur Rothstein, 1939.

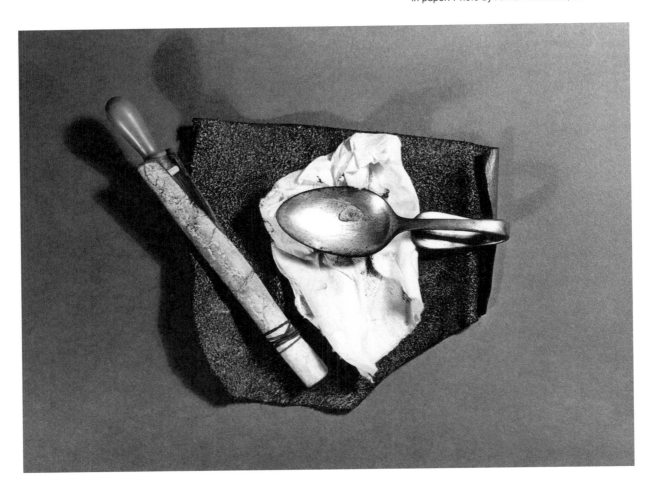

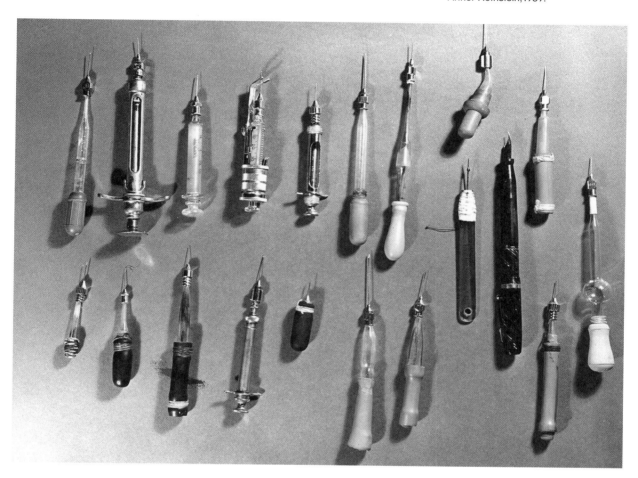

Hypodermic syringes confiscated during admissions. Note that one was elegantly disguised as a fountain pen. Photo by Arthur Rothstein, 1939.

An actor poses as a voluntary patient being photographed during admission to Narco. Photo by Arthur Rothstein, 1939.

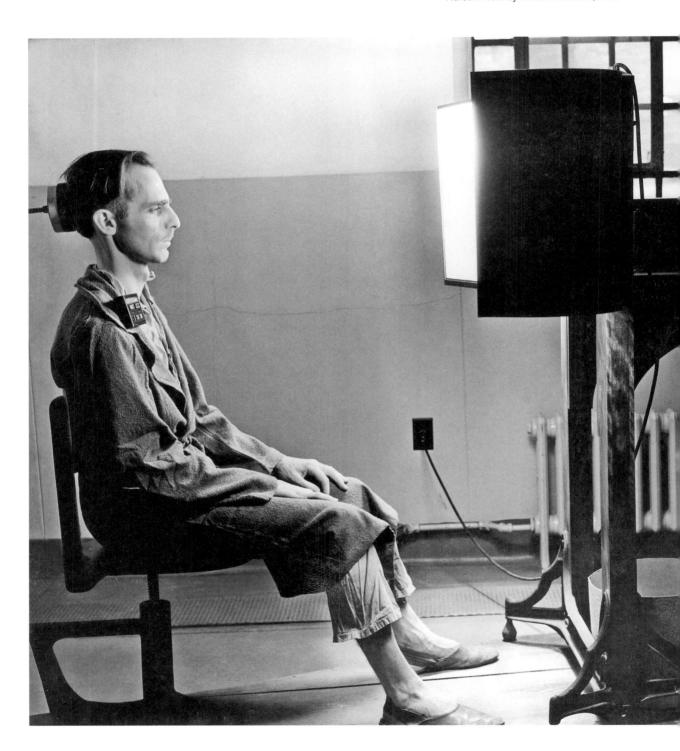

The actor in this mug shot was, in fact, a member of the Narcotic Farm's medical staff. Photo by Arthur Rothstein, 1939.

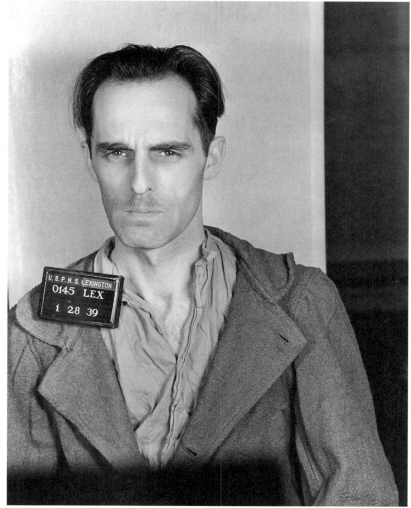

A patient undergoes withdrawal in the institution's "shooting gallery." Photo by Robert E. Stigers for the *New York World-Telegram and Sun*, December 19, 1951.

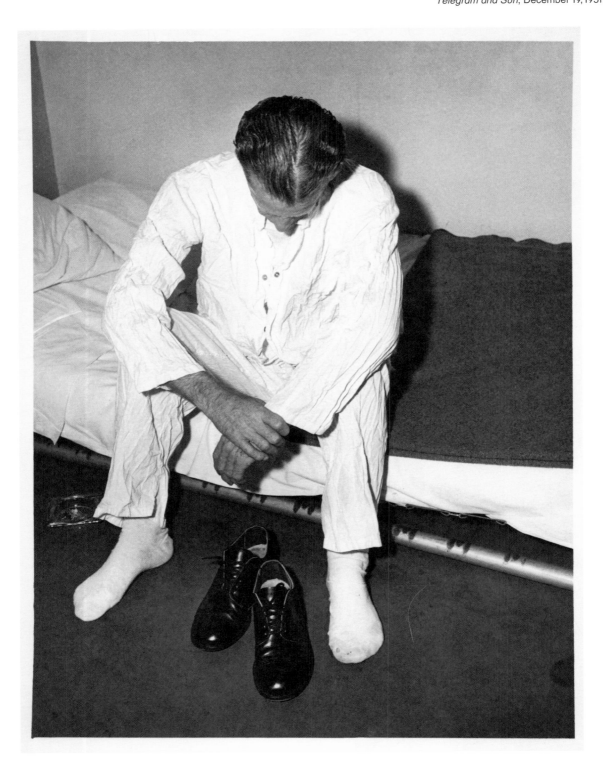

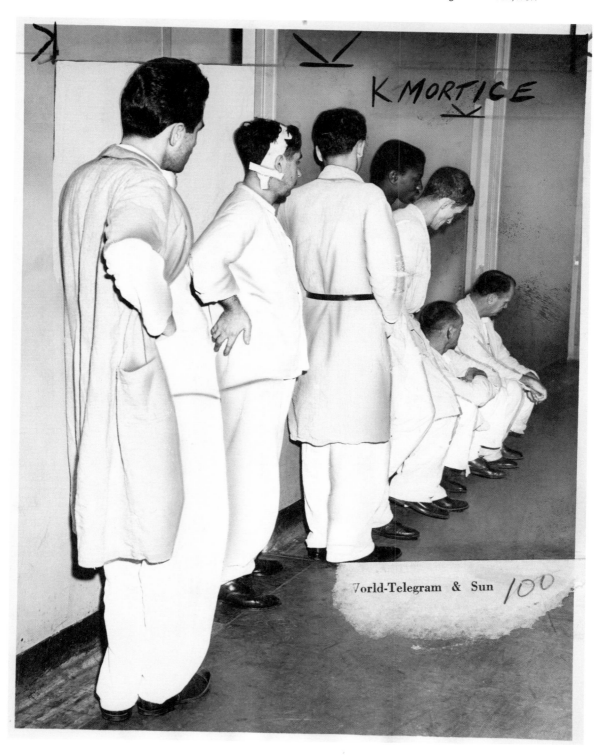

Newly admitted patients line up for a shot of morphine during detoxification. The second man from the left, with his head bandaged, reportedly injured himself falling out of bed during withdrawal. The image shows a photo editor's cropping marks and retouching. Photo by Robert E. Stigers for the *New York World-Telegram and Sun*, 1951.

K MORTICE

World-Telegram & Sun 100

Continuous "flow baths" were used to quiet and soothe the nerves of patients in withdrawal. One published account noted that the "soothing talk of the controls operator is almost as effective in reassuring the sufferer" as the flow bath itself. Photo by Arthur Rothstein, 1939.

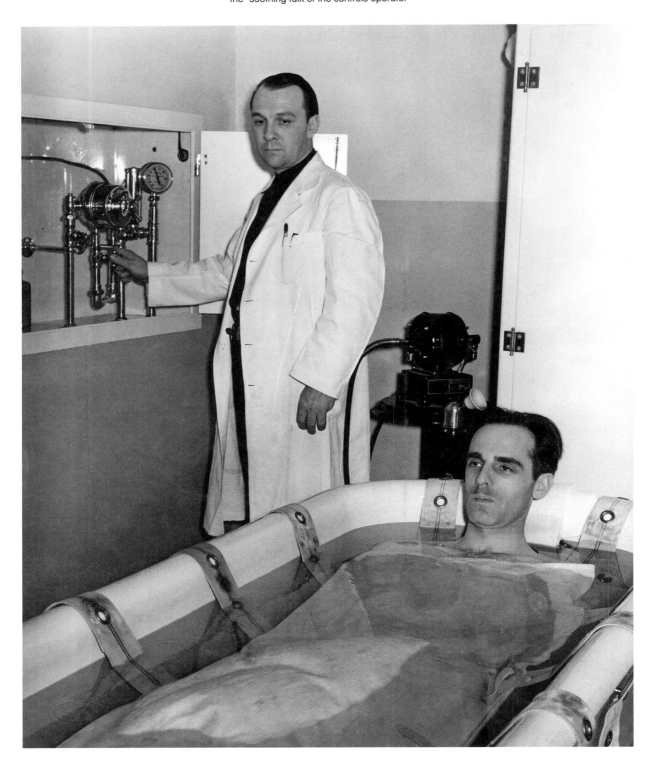

Manicures and pedicures were part of the early program to improve patients' personal hygiene and were considered part of "the cure." One Narco inmate who'd been transferred from Leavenworth enthused in a 1935 newspaper story that "the courteous treatment that we discovered at the farm seemed too good to be true." Ca. 1940s.

85

This 1951 photo appeared in newspapers across the country. One caption read: "Sweating it out after the withdrawal phase, a 17-year-old sits despondently on her bed, fighting the craving. Out of curiosity because others in her crowd took it, she smoked marijuana at 13 for a bang, then took heroin 'for a lift.'" October 24, 1951.

The Narcotic Farm / The Lexington Cure

05

The Fantastic Lodge

Young and old, black and white, Latino and Chinese, straight and gay—Lexington's ever-changing population of drug users mirrored the diversity of the US as a whole. Urban, working-class male and female addicts were always well represented inside the institution. But the population also included southern farmers and itinerant workers who had become addicted to opiate-laced medications such as Dilaudid. "The people in the narcotics hospital were from every walk of life," recalls Daniel Wikler, who grew up on the grounds as the child of a Narco employee. "But they weren't a random sample. Rarely did they have stable marriages with children. They were different from 'Ozzie and Harriet' kind of Americans."

And yet, even lawyers, bankers, psychiatrists, and ministers found their way to Lexington. An estimated 15 percent of those sent there were successful professionals with a drug habit, including doctors and nurses who had become addicted in part because their profession offered easy access to narcotics. Upper-crust addicts, including genteel women hooked on prescription drugs, also spent time there.

Women were first admitted to the institution in 1941 when a separate women's building, known officially as Kolb Hall and unofficially as the "Jenny Barn," was built for them within a quarter of a mile of the main building. But the post–World War II heroin epidemic caused a sharp rise in Narco's female population and just a few years after Kolb Hall opened it could no longer contain its intended cohort. Women were then moved to an isolated wing of the main institution. While contact between men and women was prohibited, romantic entanglements were common, as was the occasional pregnancy.

As Janet Clark describes it in her 1961 memoir of heroin addiction, *The Fantastic Lodge*, the seemingly different southern "country" addicts and northern "city girls" shared one thing in common—they were all junkies. Of her volunteer experience at the Narcotic Farm, Clark observed that being there was "like belonging to some fantastic lodge." As it happened, decades of gathering tens of thousands of heroin addicts from across the country and placing them into one centralized institution had unintended consequences: Lexington became America's de facto university for educating illicit drug users. Here, addicts educated one another on where to get good dope, how to run a con, how to dodge drug agents, who to trust, and who to avoid. Once envisioned as a retreat from the streets, Narco became legendary within the junkie subculture as a den filled with fellow "vipers."

Medical Officer in Charge Dr. Murray Diamond welcomes new arrivals during orientation in the center courtyard. Photo by Douglas Jones, 1953.

Patient's room. Narco began with a goal to both incarcerate and rehabilitate drug offenders. Yet, throughout its history the institution was seen as hardening against those it was charged to help. Former patient Bernie Kolb: "When I arrived at Lexington in the tail end of 1964 the place felt like a penitentiary. It was a punitive institution."

A newly arrived patient encounters a Narco staff member. Photo by Bill Strode, 1966.

Former staff and patients remember Narco
"as more like a prison than any hospital,
but more like a hospital than any prison."
Photo by Bill Strode, 1966.

Mess hall. Narco had a reputation for good food. Even the preternaturally tart William S. Burroughs remarked that when he was at Lexington in 1948 the food was excellent. Photo by Douglas Jones, 1953.

Inside the women's building. Patients, photographed as part of a six-part series on heroin addiction that appeared in the daily *New York World-Telegram and Sun*, turn away from the camera to protect their identities. 1951.

Patient dayroom. Cigarette smoking—not yet considered addictive—was ubiquitous among both patients and staff. Photo by Harold Rhodenbaugh for Louisville's *Courier Journal*, 1942.

Four prisoners in the informers' ward. The headline from the *New York World-Telegram and Sun* reads: "Narco Guards the Squealers." Text from the original newspaper story reads: "The huge federal prison hospital for drug addicts harbors 30 'long-tailed rats'—the dope underworld's appellation for informers. They cringe behind steel partitions of the 'informers ward' in fear of the death sentence passed upon them by the underworld." Photo by Robert E. Stigers, 1951.

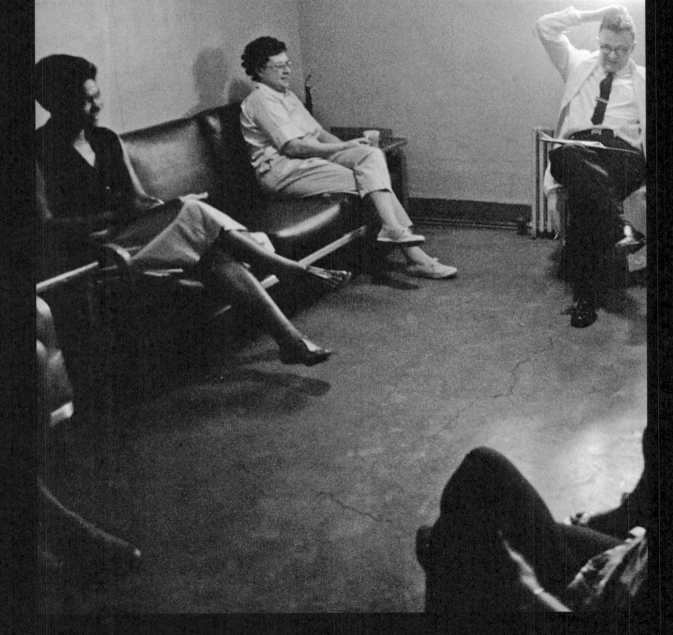

The Talking Cure

When Dr. Lawrence Kolb was appointed chief medical officer of the Narcotic Farm in 1935, he had already established himself as a leading advocate for the humane treatment of drug addicts. Kolb believed that most addicts were driven to use narcotics because of emotional difficulties and that their addictions were curable if the underlying psychological causes were addressed. Having spent years screening military recruits for mental illness, Kolb gained expertise in assessing personality disorders, which enabled him to design a classification system for sorting patients into groups that reflected the perceived severity of their psychological illness. This system, the "K Classification," was the first set of diagnostic criteria for assessing addiction and systematizing, in a scientific manner, the evaluation of patients. It was used for decades at the Narcotic Farm.

Psychotherapy—administered in individual or group sessions at Lexington—was the doctors' tool of choice to adjust the maladjusted. But Narco's treatment capacity was limited; there were never more than one or two psychiatrists per 100 patients, so group therapy, rather than individual therapy, became the norm. Psychiatrists and counselors routinely encountered resistance and bad faith in patients, who resented them for their authority, race, or class.

But even for patients committed to giving up drugs, hard-won personal insights gained through psychotherapy were rarely enough to combat their addiction. Former patient David Deitch, who later became a leading authority on drug treatment, has positive recollections of his weekly psychiatric sessions. "I felt that at last I had someone I could talk to," Deitch says. "Someone who could understand some of the things that I'd gone through." Yet as Deitch recalls, he relapsed within a day of his release from the institution: "Despite all the progress I had made toward understanding the causes of my involvement with drugs, it wasn't enough."

Lexington's approaches to therapeutic treatment evolved as time wore on. In the 1950s, for instance, a type of treatment known as "milieu therapy" took hold, whereby everyone in the prison environment—including detox specialists, guards, janitors, and health aides—contributed to reinforcing the value of the treatments being offered, which included work therapy, recreation, and living in an environment where drugs were not easily available.

In the mid-1960s, the Narcotic Addict Rehabilitation Act prompted other changes. Between 1968 and 1973, men and women who qualified could serve six months of civil commitment for drug treatment in lieu of jail. In many cases, young people who had run afoul of the law because of drugs could have their criminal record expunged if they sought treatment. Overnight, Lexington became one of the nation's main centers for the civil commitment program, as people from all over the country opted for treatment over incarceration.

Narco cut down prison bars and let patients put up beads and curtains. "Patients" and "inmates" were now "residents" who didn't live in the "population" but rather in "therapeutic communities," which they organized inside the institution. Rules were relaxed in hopes that more freedom would lead to more open acceptance of treatment. Patient-directed rehabilitation, modeled after well-publicized therapeutic communities such as Synanon and Daytop Village, became the main treatment in what was no longer a prison but a "federal correctional institute."

Institutional support for therapeutic communities culminated in the formation of five "houses" on Narco's grounds. Three of these houses, Excelsior, Numen, and Ascension, were set up in separate wings of the main building. YOUnity House opened in a separate building, as did Matrix House, the only coed house. The most experimental and ideological of the houses, Matrix had no staff, little oversight, and was allowed to recruit members from the outside community—called "squares"—to live communally with recovering addicts. Jon Wildes, a former heroin addict who had previously spent time at the institution as a convict, was hired by the federal government to run the facility.

Today, Matrix House is remembered by some former members as a sincere attempt at creating a utopian community. Others see the group as a cult that debased its own members. The program centered on a confrontational style of group therapy called "The Game," which was developed by the California-based therapeutic community Synanon. The Game encouraged members to single out and attack, scold, or ridicule anyone perceived as being dishonest with themselves or others. In this setting, where as many as sixty recovering addicts lived together, no peccadillo went unnoticed or unpunished.

The Game sometimes went on for hours at a time. Although physical violence or threats of physical violence were not allowed, few other boundaries were observed. Screaming, crying, and hugging were embraced as therapeutic. But the lines of what constituted treatment and what constituted cruelty blurred as the group leader, John Wildes, became increasingly abusive. In 1972, amidst allegations of torture and weapons possession, five Matrix House members were arrested. Wildes was later imprisoned for possessing firearms on federal property.

Despite the spectacular failure of Matrix, the practice of addicts helping addicts is employed successfully today in twelve-step programs and therapeutic communities around the world. As the birthplace of modern addiction treatment, Lexington was home to many optimistic attempts to find a cure. Virtually every treatment now offered to those in recovery was once attempted—with both success and with failure—at the Narcotic Farm.

Dr. Frederick Glaser, psychiatry resident at Lexington from 1962 to 1964, listens to a patient in an individual therapy session. Photo by Bill Eppridge, 1964.

One difficulty encountered at the institution was that those sent to Narco often resisted treatment and often appeared resentful of the doctors charged with trying to help. Recalls former patient John Stallone: "You met with a doctor, and he asked you what some of your problems were and how you felt. Basic Freudian questions, which you always knew how to answer because you knew what they wanted to hear. It was that bullshit doctor-patient thing." Photo by Bill Strode, 1966.

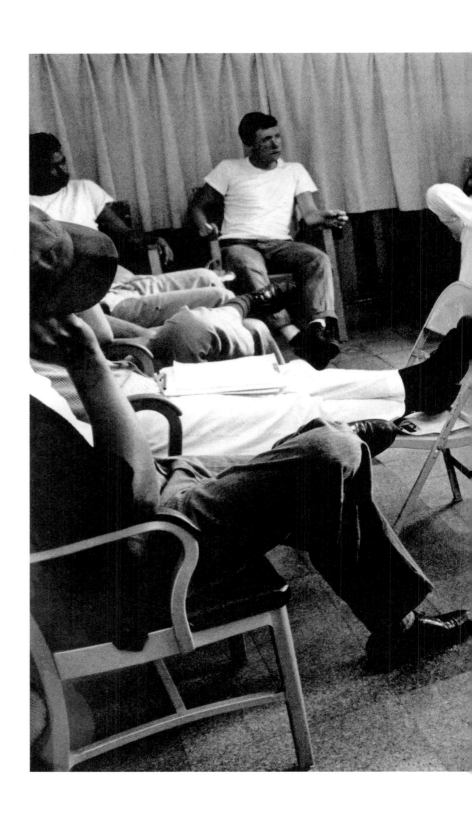

The institution held that group psychotherapy was more suitable than individual therapy for patients with "sociopathic" disturbances. The original caption in Louisville's *Courier-Journal* reads: "Group psychotherapy session yields insights on addiction. Social worker Henry James (white coat) and psychologist Bob Smith (khakis) listen as a patient talks." July 24, 1966.

Addicts Anonymous meets at Narco. The group was founded at Lexington by patients and used the Twelve Steps associated with Alcoholics Anonymous. By the time this photo was taken in 1950, Addicts Anonymous had spread from Lexington to fifty-five prisons and forty-eight hospitals.

Dr. Frederick Glaser conducts group therapy in the women's unit in 1964. Given the doctor-to-patient ratio, which was approximately one doctor for every 100 patients, it was more efficient to conduct group, rather than individual, therapy sessions. Photo by Bill Eppridge, 1964.

Members of Matrix House, one of the institution's new therapeutic communities, were allowed to occupy Kolb Hall, the former women's building, in April 1970. It was promoted by the institution as a highly successful, self-governing coed community of recovering addicts and non-addicts, but closed amid allegations of abuse in 1972.

A page from Matrix House's promotional brochure. Matrix ushered in a new era at Narco in which drug treatment was directed by patients themselves.

JON WILDES
DIRECTOR

JAY THERRIEN
DEPUTY DIRECTOR

A page from Matrix House's promotional brochure explaining the benefits of confrontational therapy.

We see addiction to the use of drugs as symptomatic of an under-lying character disorder. We have been "addicted" to stupid behavior for the greater part of our lives. Addicts are considered emotional children who need to be constantly confronted with aspects of their behavior that hamper emotional growth.

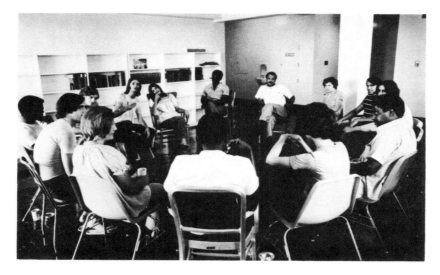

We rely heavily on the "game," or confrontation session, as a tool to force each member of the group to realistically face himself as others see him and admit his weaknesses and feel the need for change.

Other techniques include sensitivity, educational seminars, assigned readings, informal "pull-ups" on the floor, (one individual's pointing out inappropriate behavior in another during everyday activity), the "haircut" (a strong verbal reprimand by staff members), the general

2

A page from Matrix House's brochure promoting the positive benefits of communal living. Matrix House member Dick Shea recalls: "The group entity became like a higher power. It was more than any one of us. We, as individuals, fed into this tribal concept of Matrix. The house owned us. The house *was* us. And this was very spiritual. It gave us purpose. We wanted it to succeed."

Creative and artistic efforts are encouraged as a means for positive individual expression. The atmosphere stimulates the ex-addict to use leisure time effectively, and a conscious attempt has been made to revive the lost art of conversation, through which people get to know each other and themselves.

8

Members of one of Lexington's therapeutic
communities face the future together. 1970s.

Down on the Farm

Narco's placement on a farm in the verdant, rolling hills of
Kentucky was not a coincidence. Rather, the farm was central to the
institution's rehabilitation philosophy. Narco's treatment program was
conceived around the idea of an agricultural work regimen in a bucolic rural tableau. Fresh air and sunshine would reinvigorate addicts,
farming would teach them the virtue of hard work, and their newfound
work ethic would sustain their lifelong abstinence from drugs.

It was a massive agricultural operation. Patients rose before dawn
to milk cows, harvested everything from corn to kale to beans, and
butchered dozens of pigs and cows. Robert Maclin, who ran the farm
operation from 1951 to 1968, recalls a tomato harvest so large that
patients canned 1,500 gallons of tomato juice in a single day. All this
produce nourished addicts' ravaged bodies and kept the institution
largely self-sufficient.

But despite glowing culinary reviews from patients and staff and
its ongoing utility to the institution, the farm never achieved its therapeutic goals. Many of the inmates who hailed from large cities had
little use for the skills they learned on the farm. For some, sowing the
fields of green, slaughtering pigs, and wading through knee-high cow
manure came as a shock. Former patient Stanley Novick, who worked
on the farm in 1949, remembers: "Coming from Brooklyn, I had never
touched a cow. I was afraid of the cows. They're scary."

By the early 1950s it was obvious to everyone that farmwork didn't
cure drug addiction. But the farm continued on, providing the institution with healthy food well into the next decade. Changes brought
on by new laws and evolving social attitudes dramatically altered the
institution. After 1968 Narco was no longer a prison hospital, it was
just a hospital. All patients were volunteers who could not be compelled to work. With that, the farm was closed and its livestock sold at
auction. Soon after, patient protests erupted over the poor quality
of Narco's new institutional food.

Two unidentified Narco patients tend the dairy
herd, with the main building in the background.
Photo by Douglas Jones, 1953.

At its peak the institution's award-winning dairy herd numbered more than ninety cows. Here, the herd relaxes in Narco's meadow.

"Sly," a Narco patient, left, and Wallace Potts, the institution's blacksmith, shoe "Cha-Cha," a government-owned quarter horse used to round up the more than 100 beef cows on the grounds. Ca. 1960s.

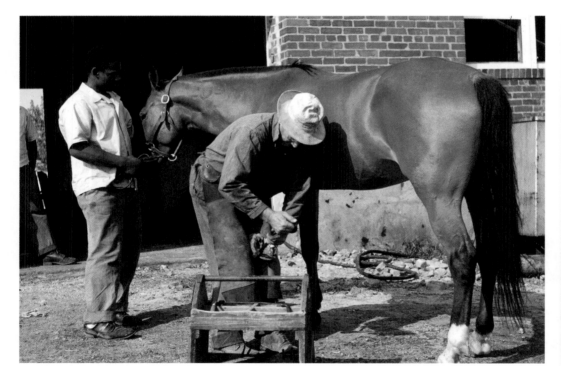

Patients work the spring kale
harvest in the late 1940s.

Top: Farm administrator Robert Maclin (top right) supervises two unidentified patients as they give deworming medicine to a cow. Ca. 1950s.

Bottom: An employee and a patient working on the farm notch a young pig's ear for identification. The farm had as many as 800 pigs at one time and produced almost all the pork consumed in the institution.

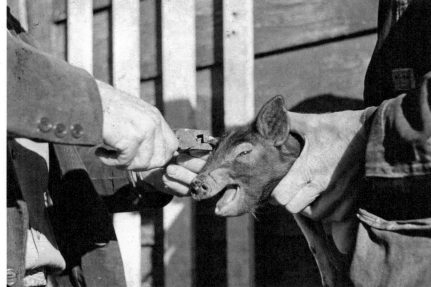

08

Work Is Therapy

The Narcotic Farm's founders envisioned the institution as more than a respite from drugs. It would be a place from which addicts would emerge "cured." Restoring a patient's health was the first step. Much of the treatment's focus after detox, however, centered on teaching inmates job skills so they could find employment after being discharged. Staff workers instantly recognized the challenges: Many who came to Lexington had erratic employment histories, little education, and, in some cases, had supported themselves almost exclusively through crime.

To transform patients into honest, law-abiding citizens motivated by the promise of steady work, the institution provided jobs so inmates could learn marketable skills. Male patients worked as apprentices for X-ray technicians, electricians, dental hygienists, cabinetmakers, and other tradesmen. Female patients, meanwhile, were often relegated to working in the institution's kitchen or learning beauty parlor skills. Patient "trustees" who had passed background checks also worked in high-ranking officials' homes as gardeners, cooks, and even babysitters for the children of the Narco staff.

The belief was that learning how to work and developing a healthy respect for authority would fundamentally alter the interior life of the patient. Pride in a job well done, it was reasoned, could override a need or desire to use drugs. But setting the patients to work as part of their therapy had another advantage: Prison labor kept this immense institution running; it also fed and clothed the inmates and staff.

The needle-trades industry was one of more than a dozen occupations for patients at the institution. This early photo—likely taken in the late 1930s—shows the needle-trades room newly outfitted with pedal-operated Singer sewing machines.

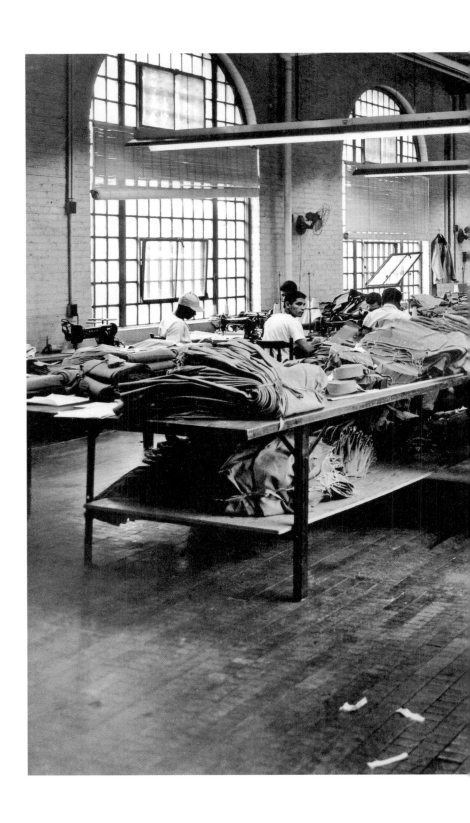

In 1951 the Narcotic Farm's clothing industry employed more than fifty men and approximately a dozen women, who made uniforms for the institution's staff and patients, as well as "going home" suits given to departing convicts. Ca. 1950s.

Top: Patients in Narco's woodshop. Photo by Douglas Jones, 1953.
Bottom: Furniture made in the institution's woodshop was used throughout the prison and was also sent to various federal agencies, including the Treasury Department and, in later years, NASA. Photo by Arthur Rothstein, 1939.

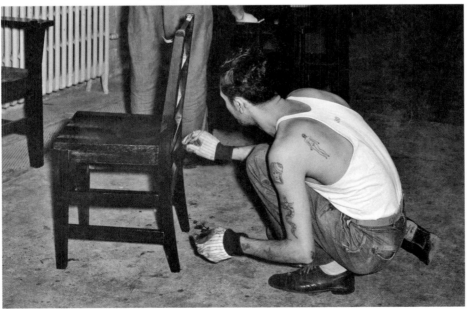

Patients working in the laundry were responsible for all the clothing, sheets, and linen in the institution, which housed as many as 1,500 men and women.

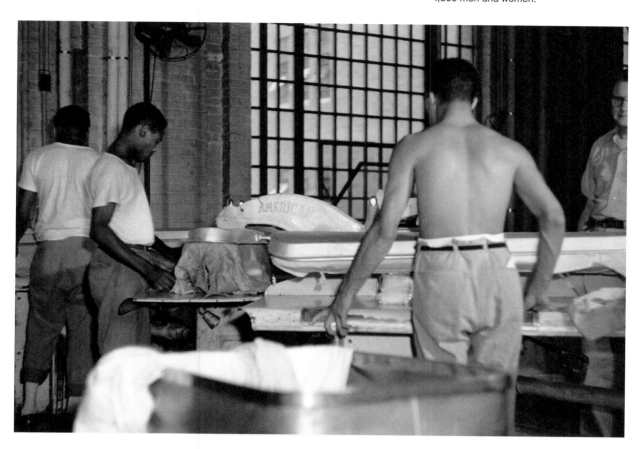

A patient tends the boiler-room furnace.

Narco patients prepared all the meals for the institution, which, including patients and staff, numbered more than 2,000 people.

Here, patients work in the women's kitchen. Photo by Robert E. Stigers for the *New York World-Telegram and Sun*, 1951.

At Play in the Fields of Narco

When it opened, Narco's recreation program was among the best in any federal prison. The institution's interior spaces and outside grounds were elaborately designed to accommodate all varieties of leisure-time activities. Outdoors, the grounds included a golf course, softball diamond, tennis court, football field, and horseshoe-pitching court. Soccer and handball were also played. Indoor facilities included a basketball court, bowling alley, billiard room, weight-training room, and rec rooms outfitted with card tables, chess- and checkerboards, and ping-pong tables.

Narcotic Farm officials viewed competitive sports as therapeutic activities that could help replace degenerate street values with wholesome all-American values. From its inception, the institution's founders reasoned that good sportsmanship, fair play, and teamwork—all degraded by the drug user's routine of deceit in the service of feeding his habit—could be cultivated in an environment where supervised recreation taught addicts to "play by the rules." Indeed, the staff took therapeutic recreation seriously enough to record the number of hours each inmate spent at play. In 1937, the recreation department logged 12,712 patient hours of baseball, 11,715 hours of tennis, 7,936 hours of volleyball, 4,473 hours of horseshoe tossing, and 4,167 hours of boxing.

It wasn't only sports and games. Artistic patients were also encouraged to pursue passions that had been stunted by drug addition. The institution offered men and women courses in creative writing, painting, ceramics, sewing, and home decoration. The most celebrated therapeutic pastime, however, was the prison music program, which featured inmate-led jazz orchestras and combos that performed for inmates, staff, and the residents of Lexington.

The institution's tennis courts gave many addicts their first taste of the game. Photo by Bill Strode, 1966.

Narco's bowling alley. The staff viewed sports as therapeutic and normative and, in the earliest days, kept detailed records on the number of hours patients participated. In 1937 staff logged 8,842 patient-hours of bowling. Photo by Arthur Rothstein for Louisville's *Courier Journal*, 1939.

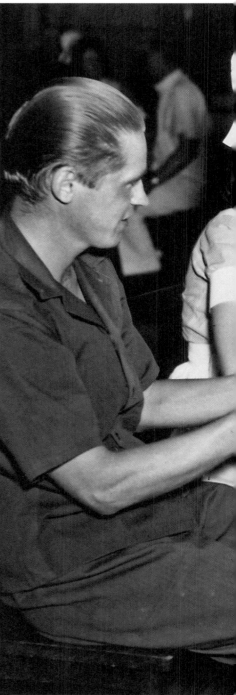

The women's recreation program included arts and crafts such as basket weaving, taught here by Mary Phillips, supervisor of the psychiatric aides. Photo by Joe Reister for Louisville's *Courier Journal*, 1951.

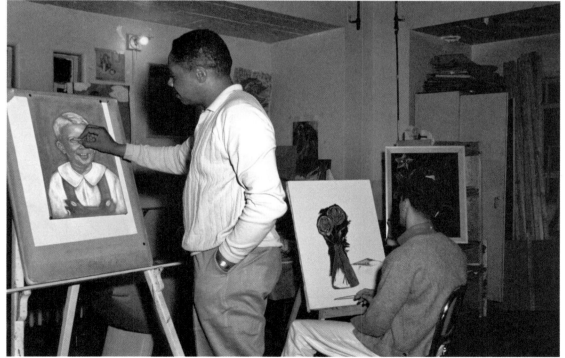

Women's softball. Team sports were
believed to promote camaraderie and
good values. Photo by Bill Strode, 1966.

10

The Greatest Band
You Never Heard

By the mid-1950s Lexington had become an elite fraternity for addicts as well as the epicenter of drug culture in America. The soundtrack of the new junkie subculture was jazz, and some of this country's best jazz was played at Narco.

Heroin and jazz were so closely linked that many distinguished artists of the era—Cab Calloway, Dizzy Gillespie, and Duke Ellington, and others—spoke bitterly to the press about how the drug was devastating a generation of gifted musicians and how these musicians, desperate for heroin, were easy marks for law enforcement. Less openly discussed by those in the scene was the fact that some players, pressured by draconian drug laws of the time, avoided arrest by becoming informants who in turn helped imprison their peers.

Along the way many musicians spent a few days, a few weeks, or even years at the Lexington narcotics hospital. The list of jazz players at Lex reads like a who's who of the genre: Chet Baker, Elvin Jones, Stan Levey, Jackie McLean, Red Rodney, Sonny Rollins, and many others. In fact, among jazz fans the institution soon acquired a reputation as a workshop for musicians. On the streets of New York and Chicago, the lore was that young musicians were checking themselves into the notorious institution merely for the opportunity to sit in with the masters. Even Frank Sinatra's character "Frankie Machine" in *The Man with the Golden Arm* begins the film by excitedly telling his pals that he's just returned from the Lexington hospital. Now clean, Sinatra's character describes Narco as a compassionate place whose treatment regimen embraces musicians, a place where prison doctors encouraged him to play drums as part of his therapy.

This Hollywood portrayal is more accurate than not. Throughout its history, Narco supplied musicians with serviceable instruments, practice rooms, and an audience of incarcerated addicts eager to pack the institution's 1,300-seat theater for spectacular inmate-produced shows featuring a variety of big bands and combos. At one time there were as many as half a dozen jazz combos performing inside the institution. The shows were a source of joy for the inmates, the staff, and even hip locals from Lexington who came to hear big-city jazz right at home in Kentucky.

"The first time I went there I heard Tadd Dameron, Sonny Stitt, Joe Guy, and many others," recalls Byron Romanowitz, a Lexington-based musician who watched several prison jazz shows in the late 1940s and 1950s. "Their big band was an all-star group, there's no question about it."

Regrettably, there are no known recordings of the prison jazz bands that played at Lexington; the only legacy is in recollections, photographs, and snippets of silent films. But for one night in 1964 the swinging sounds of jazz at Lex filled living rooms across the country. An orchestra made up of Lexington patients performed for the nation on Johnny Carson's *The Tonight Show*. It was the highest-profile gig in the prison's history, but mainstream fame was fleeting: The tapes from this broadcast were accidentally erased decades ago. It was the greatest band you never heard.

New York World-Telegram and Sun photograph. The original caption reads: "The brighter side of Narco—a jam session by patients who formed their own orchestra." 1951.

156

Top: A trombonist studies the score in a practice room. Photo by Bill Strode, 1966. **Bottom:** Unidentified trumpeter. Former patient Stan Novick recalls: "You could go to a show and see some of the great, great jazz musicians of our time. They became legends. But at the time they were just more drug addicts." Photo by Bill Strode, 1966.

Practice room. Instruments were provided by the institution and musicians were encouraged to practice up to six hours a day. Photo by Bill Strode, 1966.

Male and female patients perform a Latin dance accompanied by Narco's big band. Former patient Eddie Flowers recalls: "We used to put on a big extravaganza with sets and everything. It was one of the good times down there in Lexington, Kentucky. And everybody came to the show—the females, the personnel, the males, you know. For that couple of hours we were just in a whole other space and time."

The Narcotic Farm / The Greatest Band You Never Heard

An unidentified jazz singer stands alone in the spotlight during a 1964 performance in Narco's auditorium. Photo by Bill Eppridge, 1964.

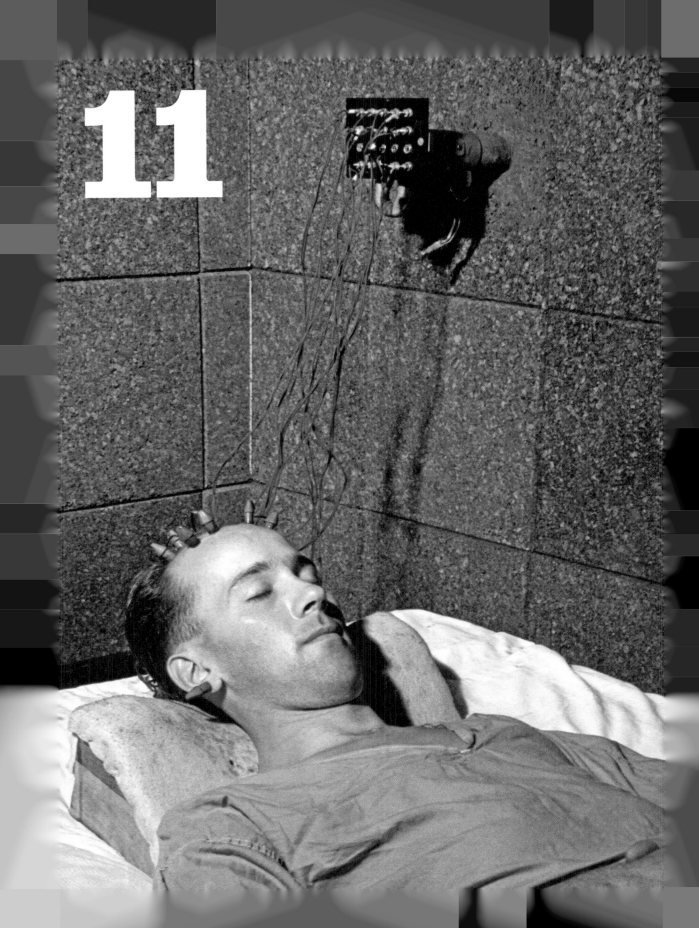

11

The Addiction Research Center

Page 162: Patient in a drug study. The
contacts adhered to this inmate's head are
recording brain waves to study the effects
of drugs on sleep. The Addiction Research
Center pioneered the use of electroenceph-
alographs—better known as EEGs—in its
early brain imaging studies. Louisville's
Courier Journal, 1942.

The mission of the Narcotic Farm was not only to treat addicts,

but also to understand the mysteries of addiction. Why were some
individuals more or less susceptible to addiction than others? What
accounted for high rates of relapse? Did some people experience the
pleasure of drugs and the pain of withdrawal differently than others?
Researchers at Lexington were presented with a singular opportunity
to investigate these questions.

The Addiction Research Center (ARC)—as it was called after 1948—
was the only laboratory in the world that had access to a captive
population of highly experienced and knowledgeable drug addicts,
many of whom were more than eager to participate in experiments
involving drugs of any kind. To be selected for the program, research
subjects had to be incarcerated addicts with substantial drug experience. The lab did not accept women and preferred subjects who
had repeatedly failed to get over their addiction. The ARC reasoned
that the most ethical and scientifically rigorous way to conduct drug
experiments was on experienced drug users because they intimately
understood narcotics, had a good sense of what was likely to happen
to them in tests, and were able to precisely articulate the specific
effects of the drugs they were given.

Over the four decades of Narco's existence, inmates volunteered for
experiments involving every abused drug known to man. Test subjects
were given heroin, morphine, cocaine, alcohol, barbiturates, marijuana,
sleeping pills, tranquilizers, LSD, mescaline, and psilocybin. With the
vast body of knowledge and data that they gathered from these tests,
the ARC's researchers established the foundation for a new scientific
understanding of drug abuse and addiction.

The ARC's early studies challenged accepted myths about addicts:
that addicts were less intelligent than normal people, that they were
psychopathic, and that one could predict who would become an addict
just by the way they looked. Researchers studying hardcore drug
addicts found that, fundamentally, they were ordinary people, not the
"degenerates" they'd often been portrayed to be. This was among the
first of many of the lab's findings that challenged popular perceptions.

As the world's premier scientific outpost for the study of drug addiction, the lab was uniquely positioned to deal with a new problem that
emerged after World War II: a sudden and dramatic proliferation of
potentially addictive new drugs. During the post-war economic boom,
pharmaceutical companies developed and marketed a wide array of
new painkillers, tranquilizers, uppers, and downers. Concerned that
one of the new synthetic "wonder drugs" would prove to be dangerously
addictive, the World Health Organization, the United Nations, and
US and foreign governments turned to the ARC to test drug effects
in human subjects. For more than two decades virtually every new

pharmaceutical that hit the market was tested on Narcotic Farm inmates to assess its potential for abuse. The lab's work led to international drug controls, greater caution in the prescription of dangerous drugs, and the now standard warnings not to drive or operate heavy machinery while under the influence of certain drugs.

Among the flood of drugs that arrived for testing at Lexington was methadone, which was first synthesized in Germany in the late 1930s as a painkiller. In its first large-scale US trial, in 1948, the drug was administered at Lexington to 115 men. All were former morphine addicts who had been re-addicted to morphine and were then abruptly put into withdrawal. It was found that a shot of methadone quickly alleviated their withdrawal symptoms. Impressed by the properties of the new drug, ARC scientists went on to pioneer the use of methadone in easing heroin addicts safely off dope.

In the early 1950s the ARC began researching hallucinogens. Among other discoveries, they found that human beings rapidly became tolerant to LSD. Indeed, after just a day or two on LSD, most patients experienced almost no effects from the drug. The scientists at the ARC began to explore whether higher and higher doses of LSD would "break through" this tolerance. As their tests progressed, they found that most subjects required doses three to four times larger than their original dose in order to elicit the same response to the drug. In some cases, research subjects never experienced the original effects, and lengthy studies were done to find out why. One infamous ARC study kept a test subject on and off LSD in weekly cycles for eighty-five days. This LSD study—like hundreds of ARC findings—was published in a leading scientific journal and today is still considered an important contribution to drug research. Yet the ARC's legacy remains tainted in the public mind by congressional investigations in the 1970s that revealed that the CIA had funded the lab's LSD research as part of a Cold War quest to find a "mind control" drug.

Opinion about the ARC varied among Lexington inmates. Many former Narco inmates recall that those in the drug program spoke positively about their experiences there and that others envied those who got into in the program because it meant getting drugs. Bernie Kolb, a volunteer patient who worked as an aide in the ARC, remembers the doctors as caring and committed, "I liked it there because the doctors were trying to help addicts. My feeling about them was that they really came there to do some good." But former ARC test subject Eddie Flowers summed up his experience by saying, "Later on I came to grips with the fact that I was used. Being a young man, I was very vulnerable in the sense that if it's about drugs, I wanted drugs."

To the ARC scientists, the ethical merits of using former addicts as research subjects were clear. After all, who could better understand

and accept the risks of participating in drug research than former addicts? As Dr. William Martin, research director from 1963 to 1977, put it, "From their practical experience they have much more knowledge about what the drugs will do than most other subjects and they understand much of the pharmacologic jargon." But the ARC's scientific methodology would ultimately become embroiled in controversy over the question of whether imprisoned addicts were truly capable of voluntarily consenting to drug tests while behind bars.

At the ARC, drug research on prisoners—which today is illegal—resulted in accomplishments that remain milestones in addiction science and treatment. The ARC developed methods to measure the severity of drug dependence and the intensity of withdrawal or "abstinence syndrome." They identified the opiate receptors that heroin and morphine stimulate in the brain. They also put forth a theory of cues and conditioning to explain why relapse was common even among those who have been drug-free for long periods of time. In the mid-1970s, shortly before the lab was closed, the ARC's Dr. Donald Jasinski pioneered the use of buprenorphine, which is the current great hope for the treatment of heroin addicts. But among the lab's most important contributions was the idea that addiction is a chronic, relapsing disease. This was the reigning philosophy among ARC researchers long before it became the accepted mainstream belief that it is today.

Evolving values among the public and within the biomedical research community in the 1970s eventually led to the conclusion that prison research is inherently coercive, and the practice of using federal prisoners in medical research was effectively banned. Today, clinical trials and addiction research on human beings continue in an extensive network of publicly and privately funded labs throughout the country and around the world—but not on prisoners of the US government.

The entrance to the Addiction Research Center, which occupied a separate wing of the institution. Ca. 1970s.

A researcher records data on a patient wired to a Darrow Behavior Photopolygraph in an adjoining room (shown on page 169). These experiments were early attempts to understand the psychological factors in morphine addiction and drug relapse. This test measured patients' emotional reactions to words relating to drugs, crime, and sex, and was often conducted on inmates under the influence of narcotics. Photo by Arthur Rothstein, 1939.

The Darrow Photopolygraph measured a patient's mental and physical reaction to slang references to drugs. In this test a researcher (seen on page 168) shows the addict words such as *Dope* and *Informer*. The patient's facial reactions, pulse, blood pressure, galvanic skin response, and breathing were all monitored. The conical microphone (to the left of the patient's face) transmitted verbal responses to the doctor. Photo by Arthur Rothstein, 1939.

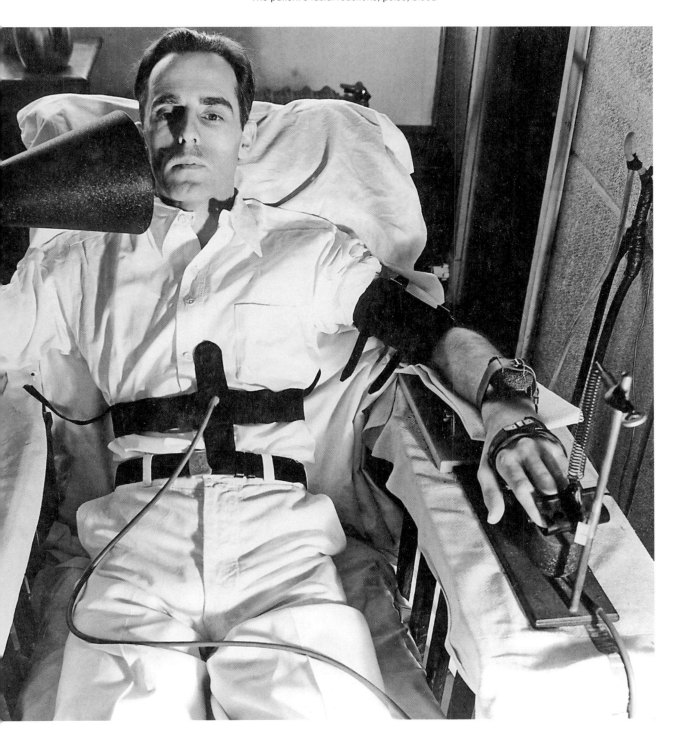

The Narcotic Farm / The Addiction Research Center

Frames from *Clinical Manifestations of Addiction*, a 16mm film produced by the Addiction Research Center to educate doctors and nurses in the diagnosis and treatment of intoxication, addiction, and withdrawal from various drugs, including opiates, barbiturates, marijuana, cocaine, and hallucinogens. For decades this film and others produced at the ARC were shown in medical schools across the country.

01. Inmates pass time playing cards after cold-turkey withdrawal from severe barbiturate addiction. Withdrawal caused days of hallucinations and convulsions for some.

02. Patient in a marijuana study.

03. Reflex test in an experiment with mescaline, a strong, LSD-like hallucinogen derived from the peyote cactus. Beginning in the 1950s the ARC extensively researched mescaline, LSD, and psilocybin to better understand these substances. The ARC was particularly interested in whether their effects could be reduced or amplified by other drugs, including tranquilizers. This interest

was likely motivated by a desire to find a controllable interrogation drug on the part of the CIA, which secretly funded most of the hallucinogen research in the United States throughout the 1950s.

04. Darrow Photopolygraph test from the early 1940s. The patient is stimulated by seeing drug-related words that suddenly appear in the box directly opposite his chair. Patients' pupils commonly dilated at the recognition of a drug-related word, a reaction that researchers saw as indicating "a commitment to drugs."

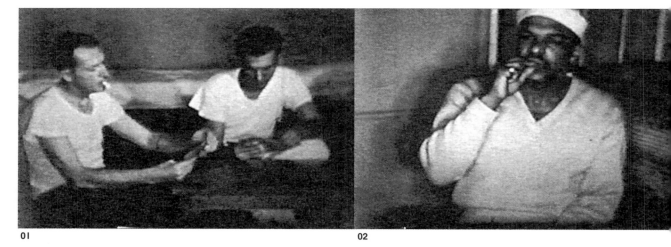

01   02

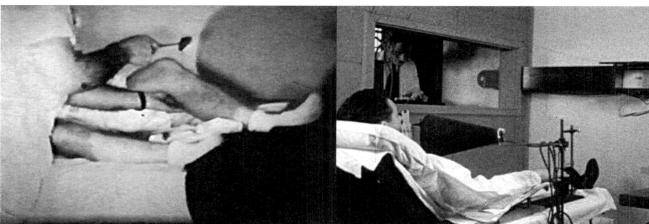

03   04

05. A volunteer in a study illustrating the condition of "cocaine psychosis," which, brought on by acute cocaine intoxication, resembles paranoid schizophrenia. During this study the volunteer was injected with more than two grams of pure cocaine over the course of twelve hours. His body became rigid, and he experienced vivid hallucinations, even catching imaginary butterflies and other insects and handing them to a researcher.

06. A patient "kicks" while demonstrating withdrawal from the synthetic opiate ketobemidone. In its 1950s tests of ketobe-midone, the ARC determined the drug to be highly addictive and recommended strict legal controls for use in the United States. It became a popular drug of abuse in Europe and Scandinavia, where it was released under less stringent controls.

07. This patient demonstrates trembling hands while under the influence of large doses of secobarbital—a barbiturate—in a 1950s study that lasted several months. Chronic barbiturate intoxication resembles extreme drunkenness, and patients in this study were so intoxicated at times that walking was difficult and falling over was common. The study revealed that barbiturates, which were widely used at the time, were extremely addictive, and withdrawal dangerous and potentially deadly. The ARC's findings led to stricter controls on the sale of these drugs.

08. Mescaline experiment. In one ARC film a test subject given an unknown dose of mescaline finds the drug's effects "unpleasant and disturbing." However, the film's narrator relates that most patients found the effects of hallucinogens pleasant.

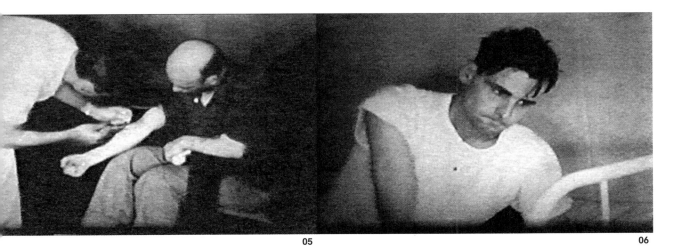

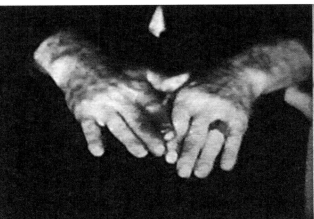

05

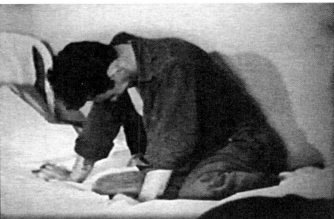

06

07

08

172

An Addiction Research Center consent form used in the 1940s and 1950s. Today this document would not be considered proof of "informed consent," but rather a release to protect the lab and its researchers from lawsuits.

CONSENT FORM

I, _____ Ref. No. _____

a patient in the United States Public Health Service Hospital, Lexington, Ky., being of lawful age and sound mind, do hereby offer myself of my own free will and without duress or persuasion to the Medical Staff of this hospital for the purpose of study and experimentation, and grant authority to the said Medical Staff to administer doses of narcotics to me until _____ (which is six months prior to my release date) in connection with said study and experimentation.

I certify that I have been addicted to the following drugs: morphine, heroin, opium, cocaine, marihuana, dilaudid, pantopon, from time to time since _____ 19___, and that I have been abstinent since _____ 19___.

If accepted for study and experimentation, I hereby release for myself and my heirs the Medical Officer in Charge of the U. S. Public Health Service Hospital, Lexington, Kentucky, and any member of the medical and professional staff of said hospital, and the U. S. Public Health Service of any and all responsibility in connection with the aforesaid study and experimentation.

In witness thereof, I have hereunto set my hand and seal this the _____ day of _____, 19___, at Lexington, Kentucky.

Witness: Signed: _____

1. _____

2. _____   Physical condition _____

                            Work assignment _____

                            Preference _____

PHS-221(MH-Ros)Lex
   6-49

This patient handbook explains rules and benefits for research volunteers at the Addiction Research Center in the early 1970s. The ARC, which experimented on incarcerated addicts between 1935 and 1976, went through various bureaucratic changes over the years. However, the research and ethics protocols remained largely unchanged during those years. At the time this handbook was published, the ARC's population of research subjects was entirely composed of inmates from other federal prisons. Ca. 1970s.

ADMISSION ORIENTATION INFORMATION TO ALL INMATES ADMITTED TO THE

NATIONAL INSTITUTE ON DRUG ABUSE, ADDICTION RESEARCH CENTER

Welcome to the National Institute on Drug Abuse, Addiction Research Center, Lexington, Kentucky.

As part of a research program in the area of drug addiction, the Addiction Research Center conducts studies in prisoner volunteers to assess the abuse potential of new drugs, to determine the mechanism of action of drugs, to investigate the causes of addiction and to investigate new treatments for addiction. Your purpose at the Addiction Research Center is to participate in these research studies and is not for treatment of your addiction problem. Before coming to the Addiction Research Center, it was explained to you that your participation in this program is voluntary. As a volunteer, you may 1) withdraw from the program at any time whereupon you will be transferred back to a Bureau of Prisons facility, 2) accept or reject participation in any study offered to you, or 3) withdraw from any study at any time. Any of these three actions on your part are without prejudice to you in any way. Through your cooperation and participation, the scientists hope to gain additional insights into problems of addiction and the addictive process.

Following admission and at intervals throughout your stay, you will be examined to determine if there are medical reasons why you should not participate in the research studies. These examinations include a medical history and physical examination and appropriate laboratory tests.

If you wish to participate in a study, you will be screened by the staff. If approved, the study will be explained to you and you will be told about the procedures to be used and the effects expected, and possible harmful effects of

The Addiction Research Center published hundreds of papers in leading medical journals, including this one published in the American Medical Association's *Archives of Neurology and Psychiatry*. It describes a study in which "large amounts of barbiturates were administered for extended periods to volunteers under carefully controlled conditions and then abruptly withdrawn." The study demonstrated that the symptoms of severe barbiturate withdrawal include hallucinations, convulsions, and seizures.

1950

U. S. DEPARTMENT OF HEALTH, EDUCATION, AND WELFARE
PUBLIC HEALTH SERVICE

REPRINTED WITH PERMISSION FROM
A.M.A. ARCHIVES OF NEUROLOGY AND PSYCHIATRY
JULY 1950

HEW-LEX., KY.

CHRONIC BARBITURATE INTOXICATION
An Experimental Study

HARRIS ISBELL, M.D.

SOL ALTSCHUL, M.D.

C. H. KORNETSKY, A.B.

A. J. EISENMAN, Ph.D.

H. G. FLANARY, M.S.
AND
H. F. FRASER, M.D.

LEXINGTON, KY.

IN RECENT years abuse of barbiturates has become a problem of increasing concern to physicians, various lay groups, law enforcement officers and legislators. The production of barbiturates has steadily increased and now appears to exceed greatly the amount needed for therapeutic purposes.[1] In 1948 the total production of barbiturates in the United States was 672,000 pounds (336,000 Kg.), an amount roughly equivalent to 3,057,730,000 capsules or tablets of 0.1 Gm. each, or approximately 24 doses for each person in the United States. Acute intoxication with barbiturates accounts for about 25 per cent of all patients with acute poisoning admitted to general hospitals[2]; and more deaths are caused by barbiturates, either accidentally ingested or taken with suicidal intent, than by any other poison.[3] Various articles in the lay press[4] have attributed automobile accidents and various crimes to

From the Research Division, United States Public Health Service Hospital.

1. United States Tariff Commission: Synthetic Organic Chemicals Production and Sales, Washington, D. C., United States Government Printing Office, 1948.

2. Goldstein, S. W.: Barbiturates: A Blessing and a Menace, J. Am. Pharm. A. (Scient. Ed.) **36**:5 (Jan.) 1947. Rubitsky, H. J., and Myerson, R. M.: Acute Phosphorous Poisoning, Arch. Int. Med. **83**:164 (Feb.) 1949.

3. Barbiturates Leading Cause of Fatal Accidental Poisoning, Statist. Bull. Metrop. Life Insur. Co. **29**:7 (Aug.) 1948. Accident Fatalities in the United States, 1946, Vital Statistics Special Reports, National Summaries, Federal Security Agency, United States Public Health Service, National Office of Vital Statistics, vol. 29, no. 15, 1949. Trichter, J. C.: Control over the Distribution of Barbiturates and Their Public Health Importance, J. Quart. Bull. A., Food and Drug Officials **9**:127, 1946.

4. Carlisle, N., and Carlisle, M.: Thrill Pills Can Ruin You, Collier's **123**:20 (April 23) 1949. Werble, W.: Waco Was a Barbiturate Hotspot, Hygeia **23**:432 (June) 1945. Stone, W. J.: 1,250,000,000 Doses a Year, ibid. **20**:662 (Sept.) 1942.

Dr. Harris Isbell checks the balance and reflexes of an ARC test subject in the lab. Ca. 1950s.

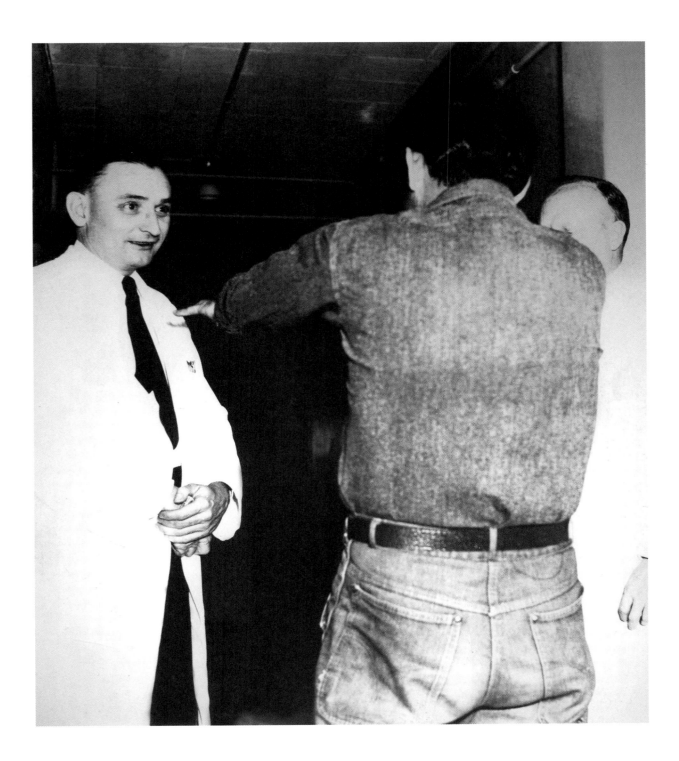

Cover page and abstract of an ARC study of barbiturate withdrawal. After World War II, pharmaceutical companies produced and marketed increasingly large numbers of addictive drugs, including the barbiturates studied in this paper. This study—along with dozens of other ARC studies—appeared in the *Journal of the American Medical Association.* 1958.

Reprinted from The Journal of the American Medical Association
Jan. 11, 1958, Vol. 166
Copyright 1958, by American Medical Association

DEGREE OF PHYSICAL DEPENDENCE INDUCED BY SECOBARBITAL OR PENTOBARBITAL

Havelock F. Fraser, M.D., Abraham Wikler, M.D., Carl F. Essig, M.D.
and
Harris Isbell, M.D., Lexington, Ky.

Withdrawal symptoms were studied in 50 volunteer subjects who took secobarbital and 11 who took pentobarbital. The drugs were given by mouth, over periods ranging from 32 to 365 days, at several dosage levels, and 18 of the subjects received the largest daily dose (0.9 to 2.2 Gm. daily) compatible with safe ambulatory management. The symptoms following abrupt withdrawal were insignificant in the patients on minimal dosage but severe in those on maximal dosage; convulsions were seen in 14 instances and delirium in 12. A significant degree of physical dependence can be observed in patients receiving these two drugs, but withdrawal symptoms differ from those that follow withdrawal of opiates and they can be avoided by keeping the dosage below 0.4 Gm. per day.

Harris Isbell was the Addiction Research Center's director from 1945 to 1962, a period many consider the lab's "golden age" for new discoveries. Isbell's groundbreaking barbiturate study of 1950 was instrumental in setting legal controls for these drugs.

Yet this study was also notoriously grueling for the study's test subjects, some of whom were intoxicated on barbiturates for months at a time. Here Isbell displays a variety of barbiturates for the *Lexington Herald*.

The "spinning chair" test provided an objective assessment of barbiturate intoxication. After spinning in the chair, patients under the influence of barbiturates exhibited an eye movement syndrome called "nystagmus" in which their two eyes began to drift apart, rather than move together. These tests were developed at the ARC and were used to recognize barbiturate intoxication and study barbiturate addiction. Photo by Bill Eppridge, 1964.

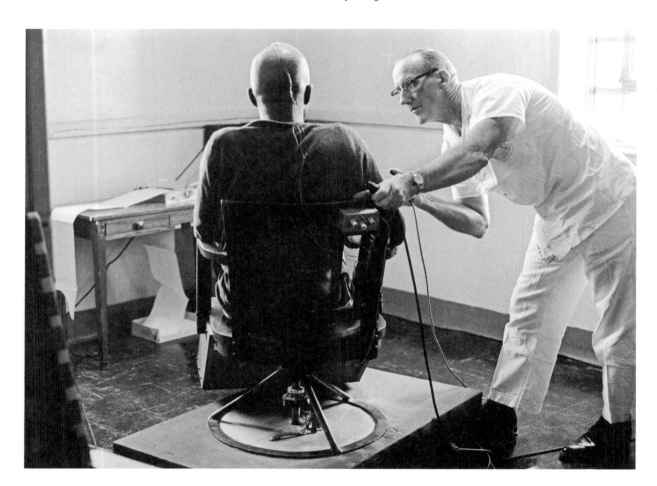

Dr. David Kay (right) monitors a test subject.
EEG machines such as this one mapped out
brain waves for studies that focused on the
effects of drugs on pain, anxiety, and sleep.
Photo by Bill Eppridge, 1964.

Addiction Research Center publication reporting a 1952 methadone study gone awry. These two photos depict an ARC test subject who unexpectedly fell into an opiate-induced coma after being given relatively small but cumulative doses of methadone (top photo). Researchers feared the man would die in several hours if his condition went untreated and they turned to a then-new compound known as Nalline, or N-allylnormorphine. Though little was known about this new drug, it had been reported in some journals to reverse the effects of opiates. Desperate to keep the subject alive, the ARC researchers administered the drug and the man quickly revived (bottom photo). Following the ARC's published report of this near death and successful resuscitation, Nalline became the standard antidote used in hospitals to save those who overdosed on opiates. Nalline was later widely used to revive newborn babies whose respiration was impeded by high doses of pain medication administered to their mothers during labor. The original article is called "Nalline— A Specific Narcotic Antagonist: Clinical and Pharmacologic Observations."

Fig. 2. EFFECT OF NALLINE ON METHADONE POISONING.

A. *Comatose state prior to Nalline.*

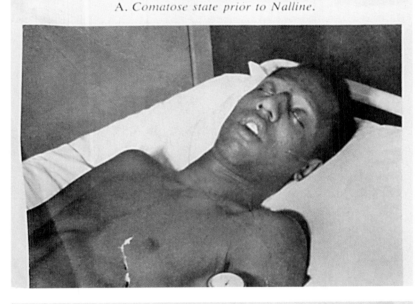

B. *Four hours after administration of Nalline.*

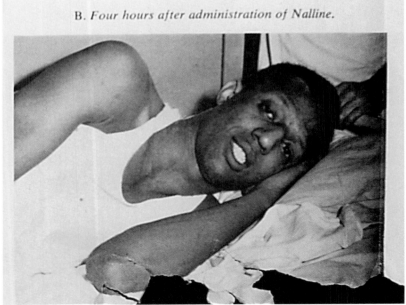

Addiction Research Center publication describing the use of Nalline in case of methadone overdose. The original article is called "Use of N-Allylnormorphine in Treatment of Methadone Poisoning in Man: Report of Two Cases."

Nalline has now been used with spectacular success in the treatment of poisoning with morphine,[1, 2] methadone,[4] Dilaudid,[5] and methorphinan.[5] The following case report is fairly typical of the results obtained:

CASE REPORT. G. H., a Negro male 26 years of age, was addicted intermittently to the intravenous use of heroin and cocaine from 1942 until December 1951, when he was arrested. He received no narcotics from December 1951 until December 9, 1952, when he received 20 mg. of methadone intravenously in the course of a study dealing with the psychology of drug addiction. An hour and a half later, he was semicomatose (Fig. 2, A) but could be readily aroused. He was perspiring copiously, salivating, and quite weak. The pupils were pin-point. The corneal and deep tendon reflexes were intact, but the superficial abdominal reflexes could not be elicited. The blood pressure was 152/84; pulse rate was 71. Respiratory rate was 6 to 10 per minute with irregular periods of apnea lasting as long as 30 seconds (Fig. 3, bottom tracing). The patient was observed for an hour and a half with no significant change in his condition.

Three hours and 45 minutes after the methadone had been given, 10 mg. of Nalline was injected intravenously. Marked increase in respiratory rate and minute volume exchange occurred, even as the drug was being injected (Fig. 3, top tracing). Five minutes after administration of Nalline, the patient became much more alert. He was somewhat bellicose, would no longer co-operate in making spirograms, arose and walked to the bathroom. Four hours and 45 minutes after the methadone had been given, an additional 5 mg. of Nalline was injected subcutaneously.

After the first dose of Nalline, the respiratory rate never fell below 10 per minute and respiration never became periodic. Recovery was uneventful, the patient being alert 4 hours (Fig. 2, B), and completely normal 24 hours, after Nalline had been administered.

Two pages from an ARC research survey. Eager to pinpoint which drugs posed public health threats, the ARC created a 550-question survey for research subjects to complete while they were experiencing various drug effects. This true or false questionnaire, known as the Addiction Research Center Inventory, or ARCI, measured patients' moods, feelings, and perceptions. Statements to which subjects were asked to respond ranged from the banal to the bizarre. Yet, this survey proved reliable for determining subtle variations between the effects of stimulants; hallucinogens; and addictive, opiate-like substances. For example, if a

1. I think I would like the work of a librarian.

2. I have a pleasant feeling in my stomach.

3. I feel as if I would be more popular with people today.

4. People could criticize me for eating too much.

5. I am sweating more than usual.

6. It makes me impatient to have to sit still.

7. Sometimes I hear hissing sounds.

8. My hearing seems to come and go.

9. I feel weak.

10. I believe I could stay awake all night driving a car.

11. I am not as active as usual.

12. I have had very peculiar and strange experiences.

13. I do not seem to be able to finish a thought.

14. I would like to be a dancer.

15. I feel as if there is more good in me than in most people.

16. My mother was a good woman.

17. Occasionally when I am mad at someone I will give him the "silent treatment."

18. Very frequently, things that seem humorous or comical to others do not seem so to me.

19. Even though I know it isn't true I feel that people are looking at me.

20. I notice that I have not been going through nervous habits today.

21. I have a sentimental feeling.

22. I don't like quiet people because I can't tell what they are thinking.

23. I am very careful about the decisions I make.

GO ON TO THE NEXT PAGE

subject responded positively to statements such as "I believe I could stay awake all night driving a car," then it was likely that the drug was a stimulant. If a subject responded positively to statements such as "I feel as if I have just done something big and satisfying," it was likely the drug was similar to an opiate. The ARCI survey is still regarded as a valuable contribution in assessing the effects of psychoactive drugs on human beings and determining which new drugs are likely to be addictive. Updated versions of it continue to be used for this purpose. The questions that appear on these pages are from the 1959 version of the ARCI.

530. Most people take things too seriously.

531. I don't waste my time worrying about the next man.

532. Some of my ideas are important but other people don't give me credit.

533. Once in awhile I laugh at a dirty joke.

534. My sight seems to come and go.

535. I would rather watch someone else than have sexual intercourse myself.

536. I am as active as usual.

537. Time is passing more slowly than usual.

538. My eyes itch and burn.

539. Once in awhile I notice my muscles jerking.

540. I have a floating feeling.

541. My speech is not as loud as usual.

542. I can stand as much pain as others can.

543. I wish I were a child again.

544. Things are happening which seem impossible.

545. My movements seem slower than usual

546. Lately I have had no difficulty in starting or holding my bowel movements.

547. It makes me nervous to look at someone who has been hurt.

548. Answering these questions was very easy today.

549. I have found myself reading beyond the question that I was actually on.

550. I would like to spend all day reading these questions.

The ARC began studying LSD in the early 1950s. Most of the studies quantified the drug's physical and psychological effects and tested the claims of the time that LSD eased opiate and alcohol withdrawal. In this study the ARC was seeking to find out whether other drugs could reverse or prevent LSD's effects. One surprising finding was that humans build up tolerance to LSD quickly and that the drug, while powerful, loses its effect after as few as two days of continuous use. In 1975 it was revealed that the CIA had funded many of the ARC'S LSD studies. 1957.

Reprinted from the A. M. A. Archives of Neurology and Psychiatry
April 1957, Vol. 77, pp. 350-358
Copyright 1957, by American Medical Association

Studies on the Diethylamide of Lysergic Acid (LSD-25)

II. Effects of Chlorpromazine, Azacyclonol, and Reserpine on the Intensity of the LSD-Reaction

HARRIS ISBELL, M.D., and C. R. LOGAN, Lexington, Ky.

The effects of "tranquilizing" drugs on the abnormal mental state induced by the diethylamide of lysergic acid (LSD-25) are of interest from several points of view. Some means of mitigating too severe a reaction is needed in using LSD-25 experimentally or therapeutically. Since the LSD reaction is measurable and reproducible,[1] it might be possible to use the LSD psychosis as a screen for predicting the potential clinical value of new tranquilizing drugs. In addition, such studies might be useful in elucidating the mechanisms of action of both the tranquilizers and the psychotogenic drugs. The purpose of the present paper is to present the results of experiments in which attempts were made to block (prevent) or reverse (treat) the LSD reaction with chlorpromazine, azacyclonol (Frenquel), and reserpine.

Methods

Subjects.—The subjects used in these experiments were all adult male drug addicts who were serving sentences for violation of the Harrison Narcotic Act. All subjects volunteered for the experiment; none were psychotic, and the majority had been diagnosed as having character disorders or inadequate personalities. All had been abstinent from opiates for three 'months or more prior to serving in the experiments. The LSD reaction in such subjects has been shown to be similar to or identical with that in persons who have never been addicted to narcotics.[1]

Submitted for publication Aug. 30, 1956.

From the National Institute of Mental Health, Addiction Research Center, U. S. Public Health Service Hospital.

Means of Measurements and Analysis.—These have previously been described in detail.[1] The patellar reflex, pupillary size, and resting systolic blood pressure were measured hourly for two hours prior to and eight hours after administration of the LSD. The data were plotted on graph paper; the average of the two pre-LSD measurements was used as a base line and the area under the curve measured with a planimeter, thus converting all the data for that particular subject and that particular day to one figure. The mental effects were assessed by administering the questionnaire devised by Jarvik et al.,[2] hourly, two hours before and eight hours after administration of LSD. The number of positive responses after LSD were counted, eliminating any positive answers that were also scored positively prior to administration of the drug. The intensity of the reaction was graded on a 4-point scale, using criteria previously described. The grade was based on a short psychiatric examination which was carried out either at the height of the reaction or hourly.

Drugs.—LSD and an LSD placebo were given orally to fasting patients in doses specified below. Chlorpromazine and azacyclonol were administered either before (blocking experiment) or at the height of the reaction after LSD (reversal experiment). Only blocking experiments were conducted with reserpine. The specific doses of the tranquilizers, routes of administration, and times are described below under the specific experiments. Experiments were conducted at least one week apart in order to prevent the development of tolerance to LSD.

Experimental Design.—A "cross-over" design, in which each person served as his own control, was used. Study of any tranquilizer always involved four separate drug combinations in the same group of subjects: LSD placebo plus tranquilizer placebo; LSD plus tranquilizer; LSD placebo plus tranquilizer; LSD plus tranquilizer placebo. The "double-blind" pro-

For forty years, the ARC's work was held in the highest regard. Here, US Attorney General Robert Kennedy and US Surgeon General Luther L. Terry, MD, award former ARC director Dr. Harris Isbell the US Public Health Service Meritorious Service Award for his achievements in addiction research. 1962.

Top: On November 7, 1975, Senator Edward Kennedy led Senate hearings on human experimentation that included the ARC's LSD research, which was secretly funded by the CIA. This revelation tainted the lab's reputation.

Bottom: Former ARC Director Dr. Harris Isbell testified that "ethical codes were not so highly developed" when he first assumed the directorship in 1945. Isbell confirmed that until 1955 the lab paid inmates in drugs for their participation in research.

Top: During the Kennedy hearings Eddie Flowers revealed that there had been a "drug bank" through which those who participated in experiments were paid in their drug of choice. Flowers had eagerly participated in the research program in the mid-1950s, but following the hearings he came to the conclusion that he had been exploited as a young and vulnerable drug addict. Flowers would go on to become a drug counselor outside Washington, D.C.

Bottom: James Henderson Childs was a patient who worked as a laborer in the Isbells' home and also within the ARC. Childs testified that he witnessed research subjects hallucinating during what he later came to believe were LSD tests: "They saw elephants on the wall, they could see the bones in their hands, they could see their brains. I thought they was crazy."

12

The Revolving Door

"If you want to treat an illness that has no easy cure, first of all treat it with hope."
—George Vaillant, former Lexington psychiatrist

The Narcotic Farm was long disparaged as a "revolving door."

One 1962 follow-up study of 2,000 Lexington alumni showed that 93 percent of those who completed "the cure" went back to using drugs almost immediately after their release. Subsequent studies were no more encouraging. One key reason for this was that for most of Lexington's history, patients returned to communities where there was no follow-up support and no local drug treatment. But as Dr. Frederick Glaser, who worked as a psychiatrist at Lexington in the 1960s, explains, "This is a chronic problem. It is very difficult to get out of. And you have to follow people up. That is why it was decided that community treatment was really necessary and it couldn't be done just centrally."

Despite its best attempts, Narco was unable to make significant changes in addicts' ability to stay off drugs. But to judge the institution solely by its relapse rate—or its controversial research—minimizes its real accomplishments. Many treatment methods still in use today were pioneered here, most notably methadone-assisted detoxification, and the research staff made deep inroads into understanding the psychological and neurological factors that can lead to drug dependency. Moreover, Lexington nurtured a group of doctors, nurses, psychiatrists, counselors, and researchers who have since gone on to long careers in addiction treatment and research. Some became heads of university research programs, some leaders of national institutes, and one, Dr. Jerome Jaffe, later directed the Nixon Administration's drug policy, in retrospect among this nation's most enlightened. These world-renowned experts and the knowledge they produced have defined the field ever since.

Lexington's most powerful legacy, however, may be in how it transformed the way society views drug dependence. Today, the National Institute on Drug Abuse recognizes addiction as a chronic, relapsing disease that many experience as a lifelong problem. This definition arose at Narco, where the recognition that addiction should be treated as a public health issue, not just a criminal matter, pervaded the institution's mission from its opening day. Glaser recalls: "It was a noble idea. The government was taking responsibility for a group of people who had largely been ignored and tried to help them." Lexington was a haven in a world heartless toward addicts. For decades it was the only place where addicts could go—and thousands took the trip to Narco again and again.

As early as 1938—the year this photo was taken—it was recognized that relapse was inevitable for most of Narco's patients. Former volunteer patient Stan Novick remembers leaving the institution early and against medical advice and being told, "The next time you come back you'll be in cuffs." For Novick, this prophecy came true. He was sent back to Lexington as a federal prisoner and would later spend decades in and out of prisons, many of them "not as nice as Lexington." Photo by Harold Rhodenbaugh for Louisville's *Courier Journal*, 1938.

Narco's Admission Unit. This photograph was likely staged. Robert Maclin, farm administrator, recalls that virtually no one arrived at Lexington with luggage, but rather "most people came with everything they owned in a paper bag." Many returned time and time again.

13

Bibliography

There are many other places to learn more about the topics raised in this book. Now in its third edition, David Musto's book *The American Disease: Origins of Narcotics Control* (Yale University Press, 1999) is the most authoritative, overarching history of drug policy. On the transition from morphine to heroin as the major drug problem in the United States, see David C. Courtwright's masterful *Dark Paradise: A History of Opiate Addiction in America* (Harvard University Press, 1982/2001). His book *Forces of Habit: Drugs and the Making of the Modern World* (Harvard University Press, 2002) makes an appealing trip around the globe in search of the role of drugs in social life.

The life histories of older heroin addicts were woven into a fascinating story by David C. Courtwright, Herman Joseph, and Don Des Jarlais in *Addicts Who Survived: An Oral History of Narcotic Use in America, 1923-1965* (University of Tennessee Press, 1989). The story of the early history of Narco, the research unit, and the National Academy of Sciences committee that coordinated research at Lexington is traced by Caroline Acker in *Creating the American Junkie: Addiction Research in the Classic Era of Narcotics Control* (Johns Hopkins University Press, 2002). The history of treatment for alcoholism and drug addiction is told in William L. White's *Slaying the Dragon: The History of Treatment and Recovery in America* (Chestnut Hill Health Systems, 1998).

Published historical sources include Charles Terry and Mildred Pellens's *The Opium Problem*, originally published by the Bureau of Social Hygiene in 1928 and reissued by Patterson Smith in 1970; *Narcotic Drug Addiction Problems*, the proceedings of a 1958 conference on the history of US efforts to understand addiction, which was edited by Robert B. Livingston and published by the National Institute of Mental Health; *The National Research Council Involvement in the Opiate Problem, 1928-1971*, written by Nathan B. Eddy and published by the National Academy of Sciences Press in 1973; *Drug Addiction and the U.S. Public Health Service*, a collection of papers and roundtables given at the fortieth anniversary of the Addiction Research Center, which was edited by William R. Martin and Harris Isbell and published by the National Institute on Drug Abuse in 1978; and *Annotated Bibliography of Papers from the Addiction Research Center 1935-1975*, published by the National Institute on Drug Abuse.

To gain a more expansive account of the history of the science of the Addiction Research Center, see Nancy D. Campbell's *Discovering Addiction: The Science and Politics of Substance Abuse Research* (University of Michigan Press, 2007). Further discussion of the history and ethics of human experimentation can be found in Sydney A. Halpern's *Lesser Harms: The Morality of Risk in Medical*

Research (University of Chicago Press, 2004); Susan E. Lederer's *Subjected to Science: Human Experimentation in America Before the Second World War* (Johns Hopkins University Press, 1995); Jonathan D. Moreno's *Undue Risk: Secret State Experiments on Humans* (Routledge, 2001); and David Rothman's *Strangers at the Bedside: A History of How Law and Bioethics Transformed Medical Decision Making* (Basic Books, 1994). Those curious about the LSD experiments will want to refer to Martin A. Lee and Bruce Schlain's book *Acid Dreams: The Complete Social History of LSD: The CIA, the Sixties, and Beyond* (Grove Weidenfeld, 1985). Additionally, more than 17,000 pages of declassified government papers on the CIA's MK-ULTRA program are available for research at the National Security Archive at Gelman Library at the George Washington University. This collection of documents was donated by John Marks, author of *The Search for the Manchurian Candidate: The CIA and Mind Control* (Norton, 1979).

Popular portrayals of Lexington are many, from episodes of "The Untouchables" to *Hatful of Rain* (1957), a film about a war veteran who returns from Korea addicted to morphine. William S. Burroughs, perhaps the most famous "gentleman junkie" of all time, wrote about his first few weeks at Narco in his first book *Junkie,* which was first published under the pseudonym William Lee. Burroughs's son, William S. Burroughs, Jr., also spent time at the institution and wrote about it in his autobiographical novel *Kentucky Ham.* The place also figured in Nelson Algren's *The Man with the Golden Arm,* which won the National Book Award and was made into a major motion picture that was released in 1951, starring Frank Sinatra and directed by Otto Preminger. Later that decade, famed author, editor, and illustrator Alexander King published *Mine Enemy Grows Older* (Simon and Schuster, 1958), based on two experiences he had at Lexington in 1951 and 1954, after becoming addicted to morphine while being treated for a kidney ailment. Writer Clarence Cooper wrote his last book, *The Farm*, about his experiences there, which was published in 1967 and reissued by Old School Books (Norton) after many years of being out of print. Also undeservedly obscure is the life history dictated by "Janet Clark" to Howard S. Becker, which was edited by Helen MacGill Hughes and published as *The Fantastic Lodge: The Autobiography of a Girl Drug Addict* (Houghton Mifflin, 1961).

If *The Fantastic Lodge* makes you eager to learn more about how drug-using women were treated in the United States in the twentieth century, see Nancy D. Campbell's *Using Women: Gender, Drug Policy, and Social Justice* (Routledge, 2000) and Stephen R. Kandall's *Substance and Shadow: Women and Addiction in the United States* (Harvard University Press, 1999).

14

Index and Credits

Index

Page numbers in *italics* refer to illustrations.

Credits

ABC News: 186-187

A.M.A. *Archives of Neurology and Psychiatry*, July 1950, copyright 1950, American Medical Association. All rights reserved: 174

A.M.A. *Journal of the American Medical Association*, 1952, Vol. 148, copyright 1952, American Medical Association. All rights reserved: 181

A.M.A. *Archives of Neurology and Psychiatry*, April 1957, Vol. 77, p. 350, copyright 1957, American Medical Association. All rights reserved: 184

A.M.A. *Journal of the American Medical Association*, Jan. 11, 1958, Vol. 166, copyright 1958, American Medical Association. All rights reserved: 176

Harry J. Anslinger Papers, Historical Collections and Labor Archives, The Pennsylvania State University: 49

Award Books: 19 (bottom right)

Nancy D. Campbell: 182, 183

Corbis: 84-85

Courier-Journal: 98, 106-7, 146-47, 162, 191

The Denver Post: 13

Douglas Jones, photographer, *Look* Magazine Collection, Library of Congress, Prints and Photographs Division: 63, 68, 69, 89, 95, 119, 134 (top), 188

Bill Eppridge/Time Inc., 1965. Reprinted with permission. All rights reserved: 86, 100, 104, 109, 160-61, 178, 179

Houghton Mifflin Harcourt Publishing Company: 19

Lexington Narcotics Farm Collection, 1998PH04, Kentucky Historical Society, Special Collections, donor Sidney S. Louis: 14-15, 21, 22, 40, 42, 43, 50, 54-55, 56, 57, 75, 78-79, 79, 82, 83, 90-91, 92, 96, 110-11, 127 (top), 128, 134 (bottom), 135, 136-137, 144, 144-45, 147 (top and bottom), 158-59, 168, 168-69, 192-93

Library of Congress, Prints and Photographs Division, *New York World-Telegram & Sun Collection*: 17, 64 (top and bottom), 65, 72, 80, 81, 97, 99, 138-39, 139, 154-55

© 2008 Roxann Livingston, Earl Theisen Archives, from *Look* Magazine Collection, Library of Congress, Prints and Photographs Division: 60

Barbara Lundgren: 111, 112, 113

Robert Maclin: 53, 116, 120-21, 122, 122-23, 124-25, 126-27, 127 (bottom), 167, 173, 185

Merck & Co., Inc. Copyright 1953. Used with permission of Merck & Co., Inc.: 180-81

National Archives, College Park, Maryland: 2-3, 34, 44-45, 46-47, 114-15, 131, 150

National Archives Southeast, Morrow, Georgia: 132-33, 17

National Institute on Drug Abuse Library: 170-71, 175

National Library of Medicine: 6, 24-25, 48, 76, 77

Office of the Public Health Service Historian: 31, 32-33

Penguin Group (USA) Inc.: 19 (top left), 19 (top right)

Bill Strode: 29, 92-93, 94, 105, 143, 148-49, 156 (top and bottom), 157, 159

University of Kentucky Archives: 4-5, 38-39, 41, 58, 59

John C. Wyatt, *Lexington Herald-Leader* Photography Collection, University of Kentucky Special Collections: 66-67, 70, 71, 108, 140, 177

15

Acknowledgments

Throughout the research for this book, the authors were given tremendous support from archives across the country. We owe a debt of gratitude to Charlene Smith, Diane Bundy, and Kevin Johnson of the Kentucky Historical Society; Jason Flahardy and Deirdre Scaggs at the University of Kentucky Special Collections and Archives; Jeffrey Bridgers, Maja Keech, and the entire staff at the Library of Congress Prints and Photographs Division; Nancy Dosch, Jan Lazarus, and Susan Speaker at the National Library of Medicine; John Robertson and the National Archives in College Park, Maryland; Guy Hall at the National Archives Southeast in Morrow, Georgia; Lindsey Hobbs, Alexandra Lord, and John Parascandola at the US Public Health Service Archives; Mary Pfeiffer of the National Institute on Drug Abuse Library; Ron Garrison of the *Lexington Herald-Leader*; Steve Nehf of *The Denver Post*; Tony Brackett of ABC News; John Buchanan of CBS/BBC; Regina Feiler of Time, Inc.; Kate Foster of Columbia University's Oral History Research Office; Patricia Castellano of Rutgers University; and Kevin Colgan of Merck & Co., Inc.

This book would not have been possible if not for the help, time, and support of many other people and organizations, including Chris Andaya, Burt Angrist, Buddy Arnold, Adrienne Aurichio, John Ball, Howard Becker, Robert Byrd, Maria Cecil, Craig Cornwell, David Courtwright, Dody Cox, Jack Croughan, David Deitch, Maryann DeLeo, Lisa Denby, Robert DuPont, Susan Easton-Burns, Bill Eppridge, Carl Essig, the Experimental Television Center, George Farnsworth, Jenrose Fitzgerald, Phyllis Fitzgerald, Eddie Flowers, the Fund for Investigative Journalism, Hal Galper, Fred Glaser, Charles and Barbara Gorodetzky, Mikki Harris, Kim Head, Evan Hirsche, John C. Hyde, the Independent Feature Project, the Independent Television Service, Jerome Jaffe, Donald Jasinski, the Jerome Foundation, Rodney Justo, Frank Kavanagh, Robert Keating, Herbert Kleber, Bernie Kolb, Lawrence Kolb, Jr., Conan Kornetsky, Wayne Kramer, Paul Latham, Stan Levey, Roxie Livingston, Barbara Lundgren, Ruth Macklin, John Marks, Cathy Martin, Anne Michael, David Musto, the New York State Council on the Arts, Stan Novick, Helen Odenahl, Marty Panone, Geoff Piper, Byron Romanowitz, Rabbi Joseph Rosenbloom, Richard Saiz, Charles Schuster, Marjorie Senechal, Dick Shea, Jewell Sloan, Jim Sommers, John Stallone, Richard Stephens, Susan Strange, Richard Stratton, Jeff Suchanek, Maia Szalavitz, Glynn Tucker, George Vailliant, Ada Wikler, Dan Wikler, Jeanne Wikler, John A. Williams, and Annelise Wunderlich.

The authors would also like to give a special thanks to Robert and Doris Maclin, Capt. Sidney Louis, and Bill Strode for taking it upon themselves to preserve a large portion of this photographic history; to Margaret Saadi-Kramer, who suggested that our growing archive of Narcotic Farm photos could be a book; and to our agent, Ryan Fischer-Harbage, who believed in the project and skillfully guided us through its production. The authors would also like to thank Jon Gertner for his keen edits and suggestions, and Brankica Kovrlija and Eddie Opara from The Map Office for designing this book. Finally, the authors thank Laura Tam and Anet Sirna-Bruder at Abrams, and our editor Deb Aaronson for her commitment to this project.

Nancy D. Campbell remains indebted to many members of the present-day "Committee." She thanks her parents, Ned, Grace, and Isaac, for forbearance and non-drug-related fun. More than anything, she is grateful to her coauthors and editors, whose energy and endurance made this the book that it is.

JP Olsen is grateful to his coauthors for making this project extraordinarily rewarding to work on; to his parents; and, most especially, to RuthAnne, Sam, and Christopher for their love, encouragement, and support.

Luke Walden thanks his coauthors for their passion, dedication, and scholarship; his parents for their support; and, most of all, Mindy for her love and Ada for just being Ada.

Editor: Deborah Aaronson
Design: The Map Office, New York
Production Manager: Anet Sirna-Bruder

Library of Congress Cataloging-in-Publication Data

Campbell, Nancy D. (Nancy Dianne), 1963-
   The Narcotic Farm / by Nancy D. Campbell, JP Olsen and Luke Walden.
      p. cm.
   ISBN 978-0-8109-7286-5
   1. Narcotic Farm. 2. Drug abuse—Treatment—United States. 3. Drug
   addicts—Rehabilitation—United States. 4. Recovering addicts—United
   States. 5. Drug abuse—United States—Prevention. 6. Federal aid to
   drug abuse treatment programs—United States. I. Olsen, J P. II. Walden,
   Luke.
   III. Title.

   HV5279.U65C36 2008
   365'.667290973—dc22
                                        2007048997

Copyright © 2008 Nancy D. Campbell, JP Olsen, and Luke Walden

Printed and bound in China
10 9 8 7 6 5 4 3 2 1

Abrams books are available at special discounts when purchased in quantity
for premiums and promotions as well as fundraising or educational use.
Special editions can also be created to specification. For details, contact
specialmarkets@hnabooks.com or the address below.

HNA ▌▌▌▌▌
harry n. abrams, inc.
a subsidiary of La Martinière Groupe

115 West 18th Street
New York, NY 10011
www.abramsbooks.com

This project was supported by the Independent Television Service (ITVS),
the Corporation for Public Broadcasting, the National Science Foundation, the
New York State Council on the Arts, the Jerome Foundation, the Fund for
Investigative Journalism, and the Experimental Television Center.